658.3124 RAE

D0228340

USING PEOPLE SKILLS
SKILLS
in Training and Development

THIS ITEM MAY BE RENEWED
TWICE EXCEPT WHEN
REQUESTED BY ANOTHER USER
PHONE (01633) 432310
FINE 10P PER DAY IF OVERDUE

This book is due for return on or before the last date shown below.

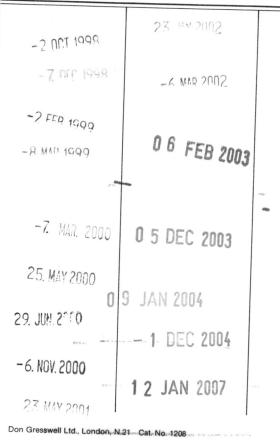

-2 OCT 1998

-7 DEC 1998

-2 FEB 1999

-8 MAR 1999

-7. MAR. 2000

25. MAY 2000

29. JUN. 2000

-6. NOV. 2000

23 MAY 2001

23 JAN 2002

-6 MAR 2002

0 6 FEB 2003

0 5 DEC 2003

0 9 JAN 2004

-1 DEC 2004

1 2 JAN 2007

Don Gresswell Ltd., London, N.21 Cat. No. 1208   DG 02242/71

USING PEOPLE SKILLS
SKILLS
in Training and Development

Leslie Rae

UNIVERSITY OF WALES COLLEGE NEWPORT
LIBRARY
AND
LEARNING
RESOURCES
ALLT-YR-YN

**KOGAN
PAGE**

London • Sterling (USA)

First published in 1998

Apart from any fair dealing for the purposes of research or private study, or criticism or review, as permitted under the Copyright, Designs and Patents Act 1988, this publication may only be reproduced, stored or transmitted, in any form or by any means, with the prior permission in writing of the publishers, or in the case of reprographic reproduction in accordance with the terms of licences issued by the Copyright Licensing Agency. Enquiries concerning reproduction outside those terms should be sent to the publishers at the undermentioned address:

Kogan Page Limited
120 Pentonville Road
London N1 9JN
and
22883 Quicksilver Drive
Sterling, VA 20166, USA

© Leslie Rae, 1998

British Library Cataloguing in Publication Data

A CIP record for this book is available from the British Library.

ISBN 0 7494 2575 X

Typeset by JS Typesetting, Wellingborough, Northants.
Printed and bound in Great Britain by Clays Ltd, St Ives plc.

Contents

situations, Real situations; Some special role play
techniques: Role doubling, Role reversal, The empty
chair or monodrama, Psychodrama, Hot role plays;
Observation and feedback: Observation, feedback;
The essential approach to role plays

DEDICATION

This book is dedicated to the memory of the late Diana, Princess of Wales who died tragically on 31 August 1997 while I was engaged in writing this book – The People's Princess and the Queen of People's Hearts, 'A Candle in the Wind'.

1
–

Introduction

Management and supervision, the training of staff in various ways and at various levels, any responsibility for staff or other employees, all require contact with people – contact that must be as effective as possible. Effectiveness in this respect has a wide variation, frequently determined by the organization in which the people are involved, but the basic principle must be related to the management/leadership/handling of people – the manager does not manage tasks, but has to handle effectively the people who perform the tasks. If the people involved are not treated effectively performance of the task suffers and the organization loses overall effectiveness. Consequently, in any training and development environment people skills are of prime importance. This importance penetrates virtually every area of work: people must have enthusiasm and motivation for their work; trainers, managers, coaches and mentors must be able to work with people and obtain the best results from them; even computer technology, although dependent on hardware and processes, still depends on the people who operate the computers. It will be readily seen that without skills in handling people modern industry and commerce would very quickly grind to a halt.

Although some aspects of behaviour are inherited, we have to learn how to deal with others and how to control our own skills in dealing with them. Some of us have a greater need for people skills than others, but most trainers, managers or salespersons need training and development in these skills. Consequently there are numerous training programmes, covering a wide range of skills – coaching and mentoring must take account of these needs; team leaders, in addition to learning people skills for themselves, have a responsibility for ensuring that their team members are, or become, equipped with a similar range of skills. People skills can be learned – by observation of those who appear to have the skills – or inherited; by practising learned effective behaviours; ensuring that whenever a mistake is made in dealing with a person or when a successful interaction has occurred, lessons are learned about *why* they happened in this way.

PURPOSE OF THE BOOK

This book is designed principally for use by trainers in the design and production of training and development events concerned with offering learning in various people skills; and by managers, coaches etc who are responsible for helping others to become more proficient in these skills, whether in training events or as part of the work process.

The book offers a general introduction to aspects that impinge on effective people skills, including guidance on communication (the prime aspect of people interaction), and various models of human behaviour and interactivity lead to guidance on techniques for specific areas of people skills – interviewing, interrelating, team operation, coaching, mentoring etc.

Each chapter provides material, techniques, hints and guidelines for presenting people skills to learners who need to learn or develop these aspects of their work. At the start of each chapter a boxed summary of the contents will save you time in deciding whether a particular part of the text is what you are seeking. Summary boxes (in double border boxes) abound, usually preceding a topic section: these can be used as topic summaries in presentations; checklists following an activity in which views are sought; a flipchart, OHP or other type of slide as a visual aid; and as a reminder to the presenter of the range of that particular subject material. Checklists in single line boxes are supplementary aids within a section or topic.

Observation is a significantly important aspect of people skills training and learning, and Chapter 5 concentrates on these techniques, in addition to there being more specific comments relating to certain people skills where this is appropriate.

Some people have a natural ability to deal humanely and effectively with others, but their number is relatively small and the majority of us need to learn to varying extents how to be successful. The techniques can be learned from a book of this nature, although reading is not usually sufficient. In common with the majority of skills, practice is essential as a supplement to knowing about the techniques. The 'safest' place for this practice is on a training course where learners can practise on each other, and learn from any mistakes as they try to put the theory into practice. A training event also provides the opportunity for learners to rectify these mistakes as far as possible before they have to use the skills on 'real' people – the people with whom they have to interact.

A LEARNING LOG

If you are to use this book to maximum effectiveness, I recommend that you ensure that the most important aspects that you learn are committed to a document that you can build up with other experiences. One of the most useful aids to learning and developing new techniques is a Learning Log, whose use should be commended to groups with whom you might be working. In addition, readers who are using this book not only to prepare to help others, but also to develop their own skills, will find a Learning Log beneficial.

A Learning Log is an instrument in which learners record, during a training event, and afterwards (perhaps while using an open learning resource or reading a book), the learning points in those events that have been significant in their learning and that they want to be able to recall. A Log would normally be contained in a ring-binder with an introduction, explanatory page and title sheets followed by sets of three sheets for use on the course, the number of sets depending on the number of days of the event – a five-day event would have five sets of three pages. A Log used in other circumstances might consist simply of a requisite number of these sets for the current learning and any future events.

Figures 1.1 to 1.4 suggest a suitable format for a Log Book, including an introduction for use on a training event. This Log can be readily modified for the other types of situations mentioned.

A LEARNING LOG BOOK

KEEPING A LEARNING LOG

The objective of attending a learning event is to learn something you can use. A complex event can contain a number of ideas, concepts, activities etc that you might wish to implement at work. It can be difficult, particularly over an extended period, to remember all that you considered, perhaps even the important points.

A Learning Log:

■ gives you a permanent document in which to record these ideas as they occur
■ helps you at a later stage think about what you have experienced and learned, particularly the key ideas you want to retain
■ helps you consider at leisure which aspects you want to implement and how you are going to do this
■ is a reminder for you about your intentions when you get back to work
■ is a permanent record of your progress and development and of what you have learned.

If the other notes you may have taken and the handouts issued during the training programme are combined with this Log, you have a full record of your training to which you can refer at any time.

Your Learning Log should be completed frequently during the event – preferably during periods which may be allocated for this purpose – or during the evening following the training day. Do not leave its completion any longer than this, otherwise there is the danger that some useful and/or important ideas or learning may be lost.

From your ongoing notes section, review these notes and select the ideas, techniques, suggestions and activities that you feel could be important or significant for you.

In the second section of the Log, describe these selections in as much detail as necessary so that you will be able to recall them later.

In the third section, preferably with a priority listing, describe, from your list in the second section, what you are going to implement or otherwise take action on.

- *What* are you going to do?
- *How* are you going to implement or action it?
- *When and/or by when* are you going to implement it?
- *What* resources will you need?
- *Who* can or needs to be involved?
- *What* implications are there for effects on others?

THE CONTINUED USE OF THE LEARNING LOG

On the training programme

At the start of the day following the one for which you have completed your Log you will, in a small group, be asked to describe the entries you have made. This presentation will:

(a) help you clarify your thoughts on the area presented
(b) help you in the recall process
(c) widen the views of the remainder of the group who may not have seen the implications of the areas you have highlighted
(d) raise the opportunity for clarification of doubtful points to be given.

As a continuous process

A Learning Log is not intended for use only on training programmes. We are learning all the time, in every type of situation, and a Log can help us capitalize on these opportunities. If you read a book and there are ideas that you want to remember and implement, enter these in your Log. If, in discussion with others, ideas are suggested that you feel may be of use to you, remember them and enter them in your Log at the first opportunity. Keep referring to your Log constantly to remind you of activities that you have not yet implemented.

Your line manager, in his/her process of your continuing assessment, will not only find your Log entries valuable in assessing your development, but could be impressed by your intent and persistence.

Remember that if eventually you decide to seek the award of the Training and Development National Vocational Qualification, this record can form a useful part of the portfolio you will need to produce for this award.

Figure 1.1 *The introductory section of a Learning Log Book*

Set-sheet 1 can be used by the learner instead of or in addition to any notes that might be made during the training day of interesting, useful or significant learning points. See Figure 1.2.

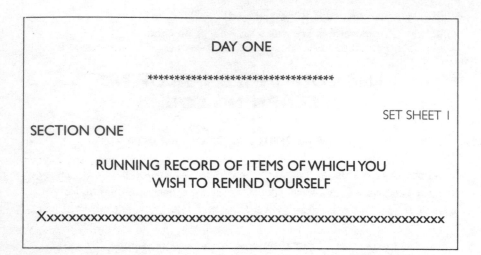

Figure 1.2 *Set-sheet 1 of a Learning Log Book*

Set-sheet 2 is used by the learners to sort and summarize the points from sheet 1 that they particularly want to recall, perhaps adding references to handouts and other information. See Figure 1.3.

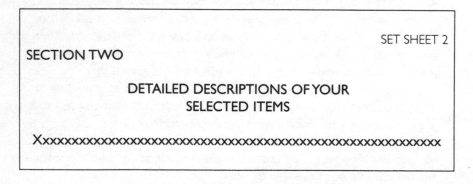

Figure 1.3 *Set-sheet 2 of a Learning Log Book*

Set-sheet 3 is a mini-action plan, detailing from sheet 2 entries about learning that the learner particularly intends to implement and how etc this action will be taken. The various sheet 3s can be used in the formulation of the final action plan. See Figure 1.4.

```
                                                    SET SHEET 3
                    SECTION THREE

             IMPLEMENTATION DECISIONS

Xxxxxxxxxxxxxxxxxxxxxxxxxxxxxxxxxxxxxxxxxxxxxxxxxxxxxxxxxx
```

Figure 1.4   *Set-sheet 3 of a Learning Log Book*

When used in association with a training event the Log is issued at the start and set-sheets 2 and 3 are completed during the evenings, giving the learners an opportunity to reflect on the events of the day and their significance.

The next morning, ideally in groups of six participants, each member presents to the rest of the group and a facilitator what they have entered in their Log, why they have made these entries and what they intend to do about them. Use can also be made of any activities or buzz groups, from which a report is made to the full learning group.

When you are reading a book you will doubtless read it in sections or chapters – separate parts of a Log can be used to record learning as progress is made through the book. Similar action can be taken if you or your learners are using an open learning resource, entries possibly being made at the different stages of the learning resource.

A Learning Log, initiated for whatever reason, becomes a permanent log of learning achieved, not only in the initial circumstance – it can be updated as your learning develops and it becomes a record of your development and a resource to which you can refer for learning recall.

People are the greatest assets of industry and commerce and should be nurtured through interactions that give as much value and enjoyment as possible. Not only at work, however, do we have interactions with people and the lessons learned from dealing effectively and humanely with people at work can be reflected in all areas of our lives.

SECTION ONE

Communication Aspects of
People Skills

2

—

Communication

This chapter:

- considers the methods of communication for people skills
- describes a communication model
- identifies the barriers to various forms of communication
- discusses the use of various forms of communication – verbal, written, visual imagery and non-verbal communication.

The basic requirement for any aspect of people skills is communication – the interchange of information, views, opinions, attitudes, values, judgements etc between two or more people. Without communication there is no interaction between people and consequently people skills are completely absent. However, as we shall see, it is rare that there is absolutely no form of communication between people, particularly those in intimate contact with each other. Intending people skill practitioners must be aware of the ways in which communication can be supported or denied and, with this knowledge, practise the skills.

METHODS OF COMMUNICATION

People communicate with each other in a number of ways, and all approaches must be practised to ensure that the interchange is clear and effective.

The variety of principal methods of communication can be summarized as:

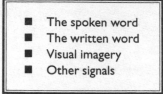

- The spoken word
- The written word
- Visual imagery
- Other signals

THE SPOKEN WORD

- Face to face, one person to one person – a conversation, an interview, a discussion
- Face to face, small groups of people (ie two or more people) – a small meeting, a discussion
- Face to face, large groups – a training input session, a lecture
- Telephone – problems of limited non-verbal communication and timing but benefits of control if opportunity taken
- Radio and television – one way communication by the sender
- Tele- and video-conferencing – brings group of widely scattered people 'together', but can have problems of identification and contribution control
- Interactive technology – interactive video, CD-I.

THE WRITTEN WORD

- Reports, memoranda, letters – all have the advantage that copies can be sent to a wide group of people without the expense of bringing them together, but problems of language, jargon and misunderstandings of words can easily occur
- Handouts – useful to reinforce the spoken word at lectures, training sessions, sales sessions
- Posters – if positioned in relevant, easily seen places can reach a wide audience, but objects defeated if non-impactive, out of date, dirty and dog-eared
- Visual aids – in a presentation a picture (including words treated as a picture) is worth a thousand words and supports the spoken word of the presentation
- Notes – if made during a presentation or other form of meeting can aid recall over a long period of time. Can be produced in a method suited to the notetaker – traditional type or, for example, patterned notes.

A common problem for all written words, however correct and well presented, is that if they are to have any effect they must be read and understood. The writer does not always have complete control over this and, unless there is some mechanism for feedback, understanding and acceptance must be taken on trust.

VISUAL IMAGERY

- Television – pictures presented can be active and current, and can make an impact to aid recall, but the communication is one way and the receivers are in an essentially passive role – not the most successful mode for effective reception
- Pictures, images and drawings – still pictures can support or substitute for the spoken word and can have much more impact than the spoken word alone
- Diagrams – often symbolic ways of accurately representing an area of interest, for example a blueprint, but must be understandable and accurate
- Graphs, block charts, pie charts, pictograms etc – can effectively demonstrate material that would otherwise be difficult to represent and be accepted, such as a complicated set of figures.

Several research approaches have shown that communication is more likely to be accepted and understood if it is in the form of the spoken rather than the written word, and pictures or images make the communication even more effective. But maximum effectiveness occurs if words *and* pictures are used rather than words alone. Modern research was anticipated by many years by the Chinese philosopher Confucius who lived around 500 BC and commented:

> *Tell me and I forget*
> *Show me and I remember*

There is a third line to this saying that is even more relevant in learning situations, the ultimate in communication:

> *Let me do and I understand.*

SIGNALS

■ Body language – which is probably the most effective and least understood of our methods of communication.

A COMMUNICATION MODEL

In any communication there is a sender and a receiver and all communication would be effective if these were the only factors. Unfortunately this is not so. Figure 2.1 demonstrates graphically what happens when a communicator (the trainer) attempts to convey information to a receiver (listener, learner).

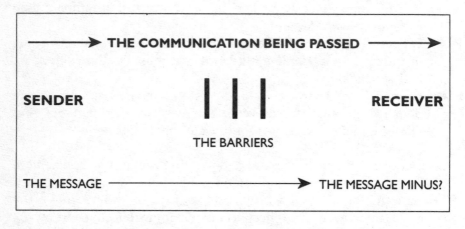

Figure 2.1 *A communication model*

The figure shows that between the sending of the message and its reception there can be a number of barriers. These barriers, in whatever medium is being used, can be erected by either the sender or the receiver – usually by both – and in the case of one receiver only can vary depending on the different individuals on each occasion. One sender and one receiver can erect certain barriers; another sender and receiver a different set of barriers. And of course one common sender can find different barriers with different receivers, demanding recognition of the barriers in each case. The sender can be the person erecting the barriers and, unfortunately, may not be aware of this. The problem is exacerbated when the receivers are in a group. Many of the members may have the same barriers, but each individual will also have his or her own set.

For effective communication, you must recognize these barriers – your own barriers and those of the receivers – and attempt to do something to avoid them. This process is obviously easier for you and your own barriers, once recognized, but much more difficulty will be experienced in overcoming those of others.

BARRIERS TO COMMUNICATION

These barriers can be considered in 'family' groups:

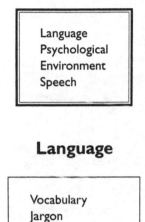

Language
Psychological
Environment
Speech

Language

Vocabulary
Jargon
Ambiguity
Woolly/rambling
   approach
Unusual words

Vocabulary. The vocabulary you use must be within the range of your listeners, otherwise you might as well be talking in a foreign language!

Jargon. It is so easy to pick up the jargon of the organization or the discipline, but if the listeners do not come from the same environment the jargon will not only not be understood, it will annoy.

Ambiguity. Be careful that you say what you mean, not simply what you mean to say. Extra care is essential when you are dealing with a multi-cultural group in view of differing meanings attached to some words and sayings.

Woolly approach and/or rambling. Keep the advice of KISS (Keep what you say **S**hort and **S**imple) in mind and the long, vague rambling speech will be avoided. Otherwise there is the danger of your listener(s) stopping listening.

Unusual words. Especially if the words are unfamiliar to you, ensure that you are using the best word, the right word, and are pronouncing it correctly. Are you using it because it is the best/only/correct/most appropriate word, or are you simply using it for effect? Is the other person likely to understand it? If not, they may feel that you are patronizing them and may react in a negative way.

Psychological

Pressures
Mood
Forced resistance
Fear
Shyness
Aggression
Resistance
Know-it-all
Too old
Status differences
Mind not on event

Pressures. All sorts of pressures may be on the people with whom you are interacting and these can detract and distract from their listening fully to what is said – work, health, domestic, money, learning, social etc pressures can all have an effect.

Mood. The listener who is easily affected by the mood they are in may be in such a mood that listening to you may not be a priority.

Forced resistance. Not every person interacts with others voluntarily, and if their presence was dictated, that person is most unlikely to be in a receptive mood and will, perhaps, actively resist listening and reacting in a positive manner.

Fear. Fear can be a strong motivator for listening and learning, but if it is too strong it becomes a barrier to listening and learning, the fear being uppermost in the person's mind.

Shyness. The learner has overcome the first shyness barrier by actually attending, but if something is not understood the shyness may prevent a question, with the result that what follows is lost.

Aggression. This may be linked with enforced interaction, an on-the-spot dislike of you, the environment or other people, but it will usually exhibit itself by an increasingly aggressive expression rather than an attentive one.

Resistance to the interaction. The reason for this attitude can be one of many – enforced involvement, failure to see the reason for being present, various dislikes and so on. 'I do not intend to be supportive/positive' can sometimes be broken down by involvement or an interesting approach, but the feeling can remain if the reason for the resistance is not discovered and coped with, or this reason is so deep-seated that whatever might be done would not change the attitude.

Know-it-all. One of the common resistances, particularly by the long-serving employee who has been put into the interactive situation against their wishes. It is usually much more effective to appeal to their sense of helping because of their experience than to try to force them to be positive.

Too old to learn. In a learning situation this is usually an attitude developed by those who are frightened to learn or who otherwise do not want to learn. Research has shown that, unless older people have allowed their minds to degenerate, they are often, because of their wealth of experience, better learners than many younger people.

Status differences. If the interactors are at different status levels and the interaction is in public, unless the group involved is well established, the higher level members may resist in case they make fools of themselves in front of their juniors, who themselves do not want to take the risk of showing themselves up in front of their bosses.

Mind not on the event. If the learner's mind is still on what has been left at work, or they have other worries – moving house, responsibility for making arrangements for a variety of events, an interview looming and so on – full attention will not be paid to what is currently happening, however important it may be.

Environment

> Noise   Heat
> Cold   Ventilation
>   Space available
>   Interruptions
>   Work intrusion
>   Restricted time

Noise. Heat. Cold. Ventilation. Space available. These are all aspects of the environment that can get in the way of listening and reacting in a positive manner. Have you ever tried to conduct an interview with the builders tearing down the structure next door or, as has happened to me, sliding debris down a chute on the roof immediately above you? Sometimes they can be resolved and the barrier is broken; at other times nothing can be done and they either remain as barriers, or alternative action is taken.

Interruptions/Work intrusion. Interruptions of whatever nature, but particularly if they bring work into the interaction environment, will affect listening and learning. Most can be avoided by preliminary precautions – a sign on a door, a transferred telephone line, instructions to a secretary etc.

Restricted time. Communication often requires a significant length of time to be effective – time to fit in the material of the event; time for different people to assimilate material; time for the sender to put over the message effectively; and so on. If there is an obvious and severe time restriction, this will have a detrimental effect on the interaction.

Speech

> Unskilled speaker
> Accent
> Manner
> Attitude
> Know-it-all
> Lack of knowledge

Unskilled speaker. An unskilled speaker will use methods and techniques which are not the most effective with which to make an impact on the listeners. Too many hesitations, verbal noises, mannerisms and so on will be noted by the listeners who may take more notice of these than of what is being said. There may be an element of sympathy for the inexperienced person, but an obvious lack of skill is unlikely to be approved of.

Accent. At one time regional accents were not acceptable in many areas. This has now been discounted, but if the accent is too strong it may not be understandable. The use of dialect words, however, should be avoided, as these may not be widely understood.

Manner. People may not be able to control completely their integral manner, but usually it can be modified for the required period when it is recognized that otherwise difficulties might arise. A patronizing manner is soon noted and rejected; aggression from the speaker results in either withdrawal or returned aggression – neither of which are conducive to good communication; an abrasive manner has a similar effect. The first two can usually be modified or contained; the last is more difficult, as the speaker may not even be aware of this aspect of their natural manner.

Attitude. This is often an aspect of the speaker which is not self-recognized, but which nevertheless may have an effect on the extent of listening and acceptance. The speaker's **prejudices** may emerge unconsciously – racism, sexism and so on, and even personal views which ignore or reject the views of others without reason or argument. The speaker may be **judgemental**, making decisions or forcing opinions without seeking other options and, perhaps because of these two aspects or other motivation, may be **over directive**. In a similar way, the listener(s) may have their own strong prejudices and judgemental attitudes – if these conflict with the speaker's, further problems can arise.

The know-it-all. The initiator of the interaction may be an expert on the subject and may in fact know 'all' there is to know about it, but listeners are very easily turned off by someone who ensures that they become aware of this.

Lack of knowledge. The converse of knowing it all and letting everybody know it is demonstrating that knowledge of the subject is limited or incomplete. The listener has every justification in rejecting someone who has obviously not undertaken sufficient care in preparation or who does not know the subject. Naturally not everybody knows everything, and at times some lack of knowledge will have to be admitted, accompanied by a firm promise to find out. But if this becomes an over-frequent occurrence, credibility will soon be lost.

Some uses of and problems in written communication

> Reports, Memoranda, Letters
> Handouts
> Posters
> Visual aids
> Notes

Reports, memoranda, letters – copies can be sent to a wide group of people, but problems of language, jargon and misunderstandings of words can easily occur. This can be avoided to some extent by ensuring that you always receive feedback when you have sent some communication about which you need to be certain of understanding. Answers will usually suggest whether there has been understanding, although a response does not necessarily confirm this – the answer may be to a misunderstood question! However, on the occasions when no response is called for the sender has no idea at all about whether the message sent has been understood, misunderstood – or even received!

Handouts – useful to reinforce the spoken word at lectures, training sessions, sales sessions, but timing can sometimes present a difficulty.

Handouts can be sent to people before the event or interaction. If the material is to be used during the interaction there may be the problem that the receiver, having read the material, considers that (a) they understand it and (b) there is no necessity to meet face to face.

Handouts can be given out during the event. Although this makes reference easier and can aid understanding with both the spoken and the written word being thus available, it is essential that cross-reference, speed of reading and/or talking etc are hand in hand and not out of step. There is also the danger that the receiver concentrates more on the bare written word, excluding the more explanatory spoken word.

The third option is for handouts to be ignored before and during the event, but given out after the event to help the receiver recall the material and clarify any points they have subsequently realized they did not understand at the time.

Posters – if positioned in relevant, easily seen places they can reach a wide audience. However, the objectives can be defeated if the posters are non-impactive, out of date, dirty or dog-eared. They must be attractive so as to encourage people to read them, sufficiently comprehensive to give the required information, yet brief enough not to put potential readers off.

Visual aids – a picture can often be worth a thousand words and can support the spoken word. However, the meaning of the picture must be clear and not open to misinterpretation, or requiring too much verbal comment to explain it. Unless the picture is very explicit it must be supported by *some* verbal description. Typical examples are abstract paintings — the artist had a particular message in mind when painting; a number of people looking at the (untitled) painting can interpret its message in a number of ways, none of which is the same as the artist's!

Notes – the taking of notes during any form of event – by both the sender and the receiver – should be encouraged, as they can aid recall over a period of time. It may be felt by one or more people that note-taking is not helping the notetaker to concentrate on what is happening, and other people, too, may be distracted, wondering what the notes say. If the interaction is short and straightforward any recording can be left until after the event; but if it takes place over an extended period, or the interaction is a complex one, taking notes is an essential activity.

Because of the generally remote nature of written words, however correct and well presented they may be, if they are to have any effect at all they must be read and understood by the receiver. The writer does not always have complete control over these requirements and, unless there is some mechanism for feedback, understanding and acceptance must be taken on trust – a common reason for misunderstandings. A writer must try to place him or herself in the place of the reader.

> Do the words I am using accurately and clearly describe what I am trying to say? If not, try to find ones that do.

> Will the reader understand all the words I am using? If there is any doubt, use an alternative word that will be clearly understood.

> Is my presentation of the written material sufficiently attractive to encourage the receiver to read it?

include plenty of white space

use **bold** lettering, *italics* and underlining

indent or separate paragraphs

---

use boxes and borders

---

consider the use of white lettering on a black background, particularly in a box

---

Is my document short enough to encourage people to read it? If at all possible, keep to one or two sides of an A4 sheet. If the document has to be longer than this, start with a brief summary of the contents and/or recommendations.

Try to be impartial and view the document as if you were the receiver, asking yourself the questions above. If the document is to be sent out, but with no feedback (although understanding is essential), use local guinea-pigs of similar types to the recipients.

Visual imagery

It has already been suggested that a picture is worth a thousand words, but images can be interpreted in many different ways by different people, eg the abstract painting. Some pictures can appear to be straightforward – eg a vase of flowers – while at the same time trying to transmit a much deeper message than the superficial image of the flowers. Unless you are trying to create a highly impactive message that causes people to think or ask questions, perhaps the most effective use of visual images as visual aids is to treat them as significant supports to the spoken or written word. In both cases a visual image transmitted at the same time can either draw attention to the other form of communication or support and clarify it.

If you intend using a visual image, the guidelines for training aids should be followed, particularly those in the list below.

- Keep the image clear and concise – if it includes any kind of text try to keep this as single words rather than sentences. The longer text will be included in the oral or written communication and a key word or phrase will make the visual aid impactive.
- Use all the facilities suggested for the written word (such as colours, sizes, font variations, speech balloons etc) but translated for graphic images.
- Limit the use of visual images in an oral or written communication, as too many will tend to distract from the principal messages.
- Humour – cartoons for example – is very impactive as a visual image, but again too much can reduce the impact.
- When a visual image – for example, an OHP transparency or computer-produced image – is used to support an oral presentation or interaction the image must be retained on the screen only long enough for the message to be transmitted, and then removed.

OTHER SIGNALS – NON-VERBAL COMMUNICATION

As we have seen, communication can be made in one or more ways:

- verbal – both oral and written
- visual imagery.

Visual imagery can be treated as a substitute for words, but there is another form of communication that, although linked with oral communication, can take place without any recourse to words. This comes under the generic term of non-verbal communication (NVC) and includes:

- non-verbal aspects of speech
- non-verbal communication.

The first-named includes the essential noises we make (or should make) when attempting to communicate with other people and we wish to demonstrate interest, listening and continuity with what they are saying or trying to say. These are the 'er', 'hmm', 'uh-huh', 'yeah' noises. If they are used deliberately or naturally they can encourage a speaker to continue or go deeper into what they are trying to say. We must be careful that they are not used too frequently, however, as their excessive use will probably be noticed by the other person and can be annoying.

Non-verbal communication includes our body signals – whether or not we are aware of them – and to which people react, sometimes subconsciously.

Various research has shown the significant impact of NVC compared with other forms of communications. The research generally shows that NVC represents between 70 and 80 per cent of the messages we get through to others, compared with the 10 to 20 per cent with verbal communication.

However, the interpretation of NVC on its own can at times be difficult, and it is prone to *mis*interpretation. Although we are communicating (through NVC) even when we are not speaking the two signals – verbal and non-verbal, if both are employed – must work hand in hand and have congruence. Many problems can occur if the two types of signal conflict with each other: which one does the receiver accept as the true signal? Again research has suggested that, where there is congruence conflict, the NVC is most likely to be accepted. The typical case is when a small boy breaks a window. He is asked whether he broke it and he responds 'No, it wasn't me,' but immediately puts his hand over his mouth as if to stop the truth getting out.

Examples of NVC in people interactions

There are many aspects of non-verbal communication, and they are frequently used and observed in interactions between people in a variety of circumstances. It is essential that you (the transmitter) are aware of which signals you are passing (consciously or subconsciously), and also have awareness of the ones being sent by the other person.

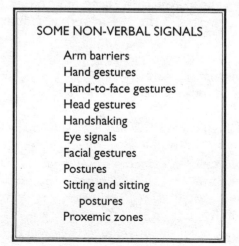

SOME NON-VERBAL SIGNALS

Arm barriers
Hand gestures
Hand-to-face gestures
Head gestures
Handshaking
Eye signals
Facial gestures
Postures
Sitting and sitting
    postures
Proxemic zones

Arm barriers – the most common of these is when the arms are folded across the chest, thus protecting the body's vital organs and consequently signifying a defensive action. The folded arms can say 'I don't want to know', 'I'm feeling very vulnerable as you talk to me' and so on. If, additionally, the fists are clenched, this is a hostile and aggressive attitude in which the person is (temporarily) holding him/herself back. This latter signal is usually accompanied by other signals such as clenched teeth, rigid body and reddening of the face.

A disguised arm fold is when one hand moves across the body unnecessarily to adjust a watch strap or cuff.

Hand gestures – these exist throughout the world – the thumb and first finger making an 'O' (for OK); the 'V' sign (of whatever orientation – although one must be careful in interpreting correctly the apparently rude version as most people find it easier to hold their fingers with palms facing inwards); the thumbs up (or down); the moving thumb (hitch-hiking); and so on.

However, interpretations of these and many others vary from country to country and culture to culture, so they must be used with care.

Hand-to-face gestures – a very common hand-to-face gesture, which usually gives a clear signal, is when the speaker places a finger or fingers in front of the mouth. This is interpreted as an untruth being told when the speaker is rather embarrassed about it. The movement may be traced to wanting to say the words but, at the same time, hold them back with the hand. The result is incongruence and the raising of suspicion. If the hand is pulled away from the mouth the side of the nose may be touched as a replacement of this signal.

A similar gesture, particularly when the speaker is looking down or away from you, is the rubbing of an eye with a finger.

Although not directly concerned with the face, truth distortion is often signalled by pulling at the shirt collar. Be careful of the person who looks away from you as they talk, pull at the shirt collar, cover their mouth while continuing to talk, then rapidly pull the hand away and either touch the side of their nose, rub an eye or run their finger under their nose!

If the hand is placed to the cheek, with the forefinger pointing up, often accompanied by a slight tilting of the head, this suggests that the listener is in fact listening and taking account of what is being said – a good sales indicator.

Head gestures – the commonest of these (although like all gestures their meanings can vary between cultures) are the head nod for 'yes' and the head shake for 'no'.

An important aspect in communication is the congruence of the verbal and non-verbal signals. Would you believe the person saying 'Yes, I will of course support you' while the head is shaking from side to side in the 'no' signal?

Handshaking – shaking another's hand can, at the same time as indicating that you are willing to make body contact (and therefore willing to interact) indicate to the other where you see the power distribution between you. The natural, neutral handshake is a firm grasp of the hand so that both hands are vertical.

The 'managing director's' handshake, with your hand facing down, making the other person shake hands palm-up, tells the other you are the dominant person. As they accept this handshake, they are accepting their submissive position.

Following on from this, an approach to a handshake with the palm up suggests openness, but submissiveness to the other, who will probably take the hand with their own palm facing down as described above.

The double handshake, when the left hand is placed on top of the joined hands suggests extra warmth and friendliness. If, however, someone whom you have just met shakes hands in this way, suspicion and caution is often the result.

Other intimate, or pseudo-intimate versions of the handshake are when the left hand grasps a part of your arm – often referred to as the 'politician's' handshake.

Eye signals – the obvious example of this signal is whether or not you are looking at the person to whom you are talking.

Avoidance generally suggests unease, lies or fear, although some people are incapable of looking at the other person during an inter-action. The more frequent the eye contact the more open and, in some cases, intimate the interaction.

It is normal for the speaker and the listener to look at each other for periods as a conversation is proceeding, but this eye gaze can signal the *level* of the interaction.

During business discussions, or others at a formal level, the gaze is usually on a small area of the face between, but above the eye level. The more informal, social level of interaction is demonstrated by the gaze dropping slightly to include the eyes and the area down to the mouth.

The intimate gaze is much further ranging, taking in eyes, nose, mouth, chin and below this.

Facial gestures – most facial gestures are connected with movements of the mouth and around the eye area. These include:

- the open mouth – surprise or disbelief
- the clenched mouth – disagreement, potential aggression
- pursed lips – disbelief, dislike
- narrowed eyes – suspicion
- widely opened eyes with raised eyebrows – surprise and some disbelief
- highly raised eyebrows – horror, fear.

Postures – the 'set' of the body, whether rigid or relaxed, gives immediate signals of reaction, and can be accompanied by other non-verbal signals – for example, a partially slumped posture, with shoulders raised in a shrug and the arms extended slightly outwards with the palms facing forwards is the classical 'How should I know?' gesture.

A forward-facing posture with hands obviously placed in the pockets deliberately suggests a power approach.

Sitting and sitting postures – how the other person is sitting can give us some good indications of their attitudes. Reversing the chair and sitting leaning over the back can indicate power and control; slumping (with arms folded or clasped in the lap) may suggest dejection or submissiveness.

The 'boss' attitude is one of leaning back in the chair, perhaps with legs crossed very obviously and with hands clasped behind the head – all signifying 'I have no reason to fear you at all'.

The square-on position behind a desk, with the person leaning forward on to the desk and hands placed downwards on it, and a stern look on the face must certainly signify an aggressive attitude.

Proxemic zones – this is one of the most natural, but usually not consciously noted non-verbal signals. Why do we feel uncomfortable when crowded with others in a lift? Why do we feel uncomfortable if someone with whom we do not have a close relationship sits close to us on the arm of our chair?

They have invaded our 'personal' space or personal proxemic zone. This personal zone extends about 12 to 18 inches from us, so when someone approaches closer than this they have invaded *our* space.

The normal social space or zone extends out to about three feet – arm's length. When people are standing talking they are usually at about this distance from each other. If they are nearer than this their relationship is probably more informal or intimate.

The proxemic zone for business space is much wider – a space of six feet is common, often helped by the presence of a desk between the two people.

Public space of eight or nine feet at least is the largest proxemic zone and can be observed at public meetings, training sessions etc. This may be one of the reasons why few people voluntarily take up places in the front row – they fear an invasion of successive zones.

3
—

People Differences

This chapter:

- describes some of the major differences between people
- describes people preferences, learning styles and sensory attitudes
- discusses problems of communication between people
- identifies the problems of attention spans and memory recalls
- discusses listening skills.

THE DIFFERENCES BETWEEN PEOPLE

People *are* different – and different in so many ways: appearance, style, manner, mannerisms, behaviour, overt or covert emotions (especially aggressiveness), learning capabilities, recall capabilities, perseverance etc. Many of these factors can be highly significant in people skills application and note must be taken of them in training for people skills.

NB

Many facets, particularly those rooted in a person's personality, cannot be modified or changed, but they must be taken into account when person-to-person interactions take place. Frequently the first indication for, say, an interviewer of a specific personality trait is its occurrence as a particular behaviour during the interaction. The interviewee might suddenly become uncommunicative, or aggressive, for no apparent reason. There is usually a reason, however, although at times it is completely hidden from the interviewer.

At this change in behaviour the interviewer must start a history check, looking back over the recent process of the interaction and in particular what they said or did themselves. At times a reference to a type of situation may be the trigger to the change in behaviour: if this is suspected, the interviewer can carefully repeat the situation in another form to see what reaction occurs. In many cases this is successful, but if it is not, and other experimental approaches produce the same lack of success, perhaps the only recourse remaining might be to ask in as delicate a manner as possible the reason for the change in attitude.

Non-verbal communication (NVC) was described in Chapter 2, and many different people have a range of these, some of which mean one thing to one person, and another thing to someone else. I have a friend who, when we meet in the street and start talking, immediately looks for something to lean against, giving an overt impression of non-interest. In fact he means quite the opposite, because if he hasn't time to stand and talk, but doesn't want to give this impression, he stays in one place, upright! Of course, many of these NVC signals and mannerisms can only be determined over a substantial period of time, but it is surprising how many signals you can become aware of in a relatively short time if you look out for them. The eyes and their movements are particularly expressive and significant.

PEOPLE PREFERENCES

One of the differences between people that is particularly significant in training and coaching people in people skills is their preference for learning and behaving. This concept stems from David Kolb who, following the personality type studies of psychological gurus such as Freud, became the architect of modern concepts of the way people learn. In the 1960s and 1970s he developed what has become known by many as Kolb's Learning Cycle, from which developed a model of learning styles and preferences. Because it represents the preferences of people it also reflects their personalities and behaviours.

The Learning Cycle, shown in Figure 3.1, proposes that the process of learning in most cases starts with the learner experiencing something, an event, a feeling, an emotion or whatever.

In order to learn from this *experience* it is necessary not simply to let the experience happen and then move on, as so many of us tend to do. The experience should be reflected on in terms of what happened, when certain things happened, who made them happen, what resulted from these actions etc. From this *reflection* the next stage is to make conclusions about the experience – what was good and bad about it and why, what worked and what didn't (and why). As a result of *concluding* in this way and identifying what you have learned, *planning* can take place about how you might behave in a future situation of this nature, and certainly what you intend to do with the learning that you have

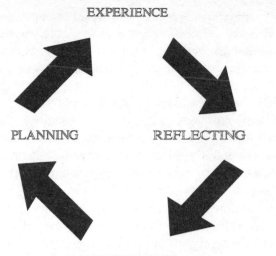

EXPERIENCE

PLANNING

REFLECTING

CONCLUDING

Figure 3.1 *Kolb's Learning Cycle*

achieved from the preceding stages of the cycle. It is an unfortunate fact that in most people event situations, the reflecting, concluding and planning stages are most likely to be ignored. Well-balanced learning events should ensure that there is encouragement and time given to the learners to take full account of *all* the stages. Managers who are to have face-to-face interactions with their staff will benefit from considering their likely actions before the event by relating these to the cycle.

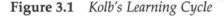

LEARNING STYLES

Similar studies to those of Kolb were conducted in the United Kingdom by Peter Honey and Alan Mumford. These two management development consultants and psychologists followed a much more pragmatic path than that of Kolb and the result, the Learning Style Questionnaire, is a more practical instrument for general and training use. In addition to identifying the learning preferences and styles of people, the questionnaire can also suggest the personality and behaviour types they have.

The Honey/Mumford approach is also based on the classic learning cycle. This cycle 'starts' with the learner doing something, experiencing something, feeling something – whether it be factual, practical or emotional. Following the experience, learning is reinforced by a period of reflection, during which the learner reflects on what has been observed during and what can be recalled afterwards about the experience – what in fact happened, how it happened, who did it, what the result was, and so on – all the observable incidents which can be stored as factual, detailed information. This activity requires the learner to stop any other or furthering action in order to 'catalogue' the reflections.

In the third stage the data collected are analysed in terms of the reasons for what happened, alternative ways in which the experience might have taken place, an identification of the most effective option, and many other theoretical considerations based on what was done and what was seen to be done. This is the stage of the theorist or conceptualizer.

But conceptualization has to be translated into action if it is to have any worth. This takes place in the fourth stage, when the pragmatist attitude becomes supreme. The watchword of this person is, 'If it isn't practical, then it isn't worth anything'. This is where and when the historical considerations are translated into future, practical action by people who care about practicalities.

The cycle then returns to the beginning (the experience), which may be a repeat of the original experience incorporating the lessons learned in the previous stages. The cycle recommences, hopefully with a shorter lifetime, the lessons learned on the first occasion producing a fully effective event.

In practice most people have a preference for one or more of these stages, and if these preferences are strong and overpowering problems of complete learning and behaviour exist. For ease of reference these preference styles have been given descriptive labels.

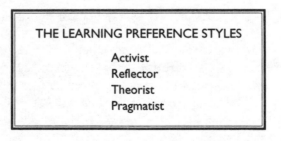

THE LEARNING PREFERENCE STYLES

Activist
Reflector
Theorist
Pragmatist

For example, a person who becomes 'locked in' on the active, doing stage is less likely to stop to reflect (or even to consider and reflect before starting) or analyse what has happened or is happening, and consequently will repeat the original mistakes or even make new ones. This 'activist' is likely to react badly to a people skills approach that requires them to sit back and consider actions and analyse the most effective approaches. They are even less likely to accept sitting and discussing the problems. Probably the most effective way of getting through to them is to give them something to do that is likely to have a powerful influence on them and so transmit the message in this way. The very strong activist will, however, need to be almost compelled, even after a powerful experience, to consider the implications.

The reflector, who is so enamoured with considering what has happened, will let life pass by with others making decisions, taking action and so on. The people approach to this type will possibly be most successful if they are required to be more activist and experience events, while allowing them to reflect on these for a period before interacting directly with them to achieve the objectives.

The locked-in theorists will become so interested in the convolutions of the internal intricacies that nothing will be done and they will probably want to sit in on the interactions and discuss *ad nauseam*. Denying this discussion will produce negative results, but it should be preceded by genuine activity, should be strongly controlled, and restrained within the practical bounds suggested by the situation.

The pragmatist at the end of the cycle might ignore anything, because if it is not a practical event it must be of no value or interest, and pragmatists become impatient if asked to consider more hypothetical concepts. An involvement in people skills must ensure that the pragmatist recognizes the more conceptual preferences and needs of others, and that everything is not a black and white, physical entity.

Figure 3.2 describes the learning style preferences of the activist, the reflector, the theorist and the pragmatist, and demonstrates their direct relationship to the Learning Cycle.

ACTIVIST (EXPERIENCING)

PRAGMATIST (PLANNING)

REFLECTOR (REFLECTING)

THEORIST (CONCLUDING)

Figure 3.2 *The Learning Styles of Honey and Mumford*

SENSORY ATTITUDES

Attitudes are controlled not only by the styles outlined by Honey and Mumford; people also react to sensory effects – hearing, seeing, touching, smelling, visualizing, doing and so on – and these have an additional helping or hindering aspect in interactions.

SENSORY ATTITUDES

Sight – reading, seeing,
    visualizing, writing
Hearing – listening
Touching – doing
Smell
Taste

Sensory attitudes that have an influence on the practice of people skills include four preferences that rely on the **sense of sight**.

1. *Reading.* Reading for information, skill techniques or procedural written material can be difficult for many. It is fraught with problems caused by the level of intellect, understanding capabilities and other considerations such as language, particularly where a number of races and cultures are involved. Reflectors and theorists are usually more at home in this medium. There is little doubt that when the words are accompanied by pictures the acceptance of the words is supported, as we saw earlier. However, this is not an easy or cheap addition to the pages of most books or documents.
2. *Seeing.* Many people have to see something before they can understand and, as a result, learn and accept. The sight might be an object itself, a model, or even a graphic visual aid or computer graphic. Seeing the object of learning avoids the necessity of attempting to visualize.
3. *Visualization.* This, too, is a difficult approach for many, requiring the person, from verbal or written descriptions, to visualize an object, event or concept. Frequently this approach is used in conjunction with sight of the item following a preparatory visualizing description.
4. *Writing.* Whether it is the act of copying something from an existing text; interpreting, analysing and summarizing an extended text; or making notes from a verbal presentation, many people find the

act of writing something down helps their acceptance, learning, retention and recall.

The sense of hearing can have a significant influence.

■ *Listening.* Those who find it difficult to take to the written word, whether through difficulties of understanding or an inherent problem with that medium, will frequently understand and accept from the spoken word. This approach usually works in an environment where questioning and discussion can take place and where the listener is willing to take part in these activities.

Although more limited in some ways, the **sense of touch** cannot be ignored in encouraging effective learning and acceptance. When considered in terms of **doing** it can become the most important sense.

■ *Touching.* Touching has a significant application in the learning of certain skills, particularly those where a few minutes of hands-on experience is worth hours of description. Where this sense is a preference of the other person, more effective interaction will result if they are given the opportunity of touching something rather than reading or talking about it.
■ *Doing.* This approach is considered by many as the ultimate in interactive processes, particularly in a learning situation; it is usually preceded by other forms such as verbal descriptions, graphical representations and so on. People are given the opportunity, usually under supervision or observation, to perform an act, whether it is practically operational, procedural or one requiring the performance of task or people skills.

The final senses, those of **smell** and **taste,** are perhaps even more limited in application than touch, but in specific situations must be considered as aids. If the smell or taste of something is significant in the processes involved with the people skill activity, their inclusion is essential.

COMMUNICATION PROBLEMS OF THE INTERACTION INSTIGATOR

The problems of communication in people skills are not simply one-sided, the fault of the other person; many can be attributed to the instigator of the interaction – manager, supervisor, counsellor, personnel officer etc. All the preferences and senses attitudes described above can be applied equally to both (or all) parties to a people interaction. But the instigator can inject other aspects, and if these are unsuitable or not applicable in a particular situation the interaction can be out of sync. These factors include:

Lack of people skills
Unsuitable manner and
    approach
Inarticulateness
Prejudices
Lack of relevant knowledge

Lack of people skills

As suggested earlier, only a few people are born with a personality that enables them to be skilful in dealing with many types of people and many types of situations. We all appear to have the ability to improve our people skills, but in most cases this requires a conscious effort on our part – and usually outside help. Without at least a basis of the skills necessary, untold damage between people can occur and the requisite action to resolve a situation not taken. Books such as this will give some of the *information* about the skills involved, but real skill will only be achieved through support such as that found on a training and development course on which safe practice is available, followed by as much practice in real life as possible, preferably with local support and feedback.

Unsuitable manner and approach

As suggested above, some of these failings can be remedied by supportive coaching and training, once the individual and others have identified what the failings are. This identification will suggest whether they can be remedied. Obviously, someone with strong personality defects has a major problem that can really only be solved by that person – an external agent cannot change someone's personality or even behaviour; only that person can do anything about these. Usually it is the behavioural aspects that are capable of change and it is in this area that development should concentrate. Someone who is always interrupting others, who always reacts negatively to the proposals of others, who rarely listens to what others are saying etc – these are all behavioural aspects that, with help and the determination of the person to do something, can be modified.

Frequently an unsuitable approach is simply due to lack of knowledge on the part of the initiator about the most effective way of proceeding in the various circumstances. Again techniques and approaches can initially be learned from reading, supplemented by attending a training course that includes practice, then as much real-life practice as possible (supervised in the initial stages and given the facility of feedback).

Inarticulateness

A lack of success in people interactions is frequently due to some form of inarticulateness – lack of knowledge of what to say and how to say it, shyness or fear of speaking to others, fear of the situation. The first of these can be fairly simply remedied by attending a training event concerned with a particular approach, in which guidance is given on how to deal with various situations – 'in a given situation, your opening statement or question could be. . .; then you would ask. . .; etc'; 'when you ask x question, depending on circumstances, it might be best phrased as. . .' and so on.

Fear of a situation can often be reduced, if not removed, as a result of increased confidence in using techniques and approaches found in the situation – again a training course can help, particularly if it is supported by at-work events. One of people's principal fears is of public speaking – this is usually really the fear of making a fool of oneself, a fear reduced when effective techniques and skills are learned and practised.

Inherent shyness can be more difficult to remedy, as this reflects more the person's personality than simply their behaviour. Practice, feedback and support, and increased confidence through being aware of the skills and techniques available can modify this personality aspect, which itself can sometimes be a helpful feature unless carried to an extreme. Otherwise, what is required is a decision to achieve results, and this can only come about through personal determination.

Prejudices

Few people are totally without prejudice of some kind, or at times make judgmental decisions based on prejudices or other negative feelings. Obviously, in people interactions allowing these to intrude on the event can have disastrous consequences. So you don't like black people; white people; men; women; blondes; brunettes; Asians; Scots; Welsh: English etc – when you are interacting with another person or persons, particularly in an official event, these feelings must not only be kept hidden but must also be excluded from any thinking or activity relating to the interaction. If the prejudicial feeling is allowed to approach the surface, a very small stimulus will enable it to surface completely and become an overt and negative behaviour.

Lack of relevant knowledge

Knowledge areas can apply to the skills of conducting or taking part in an interaction (as suggested above), or may be a deficiency in the technical knowledge that stems from the event. Avoiding this problem is part of the planning process for the event; for example, in a negotiation you need to know beforehand to what extent the organization is prepared to move; in a social counselling situation you need to have as much information as possible about the agencies that would be able to help; in an interpersonal behaviour modification event you need to know about the various models of acceptable behaviour.

ATTENTION SPANS

In any interactive event you need to be aware of the blocks to attention and recall that can occur, both in yourself and others. Although it can vary considerably with the person, with the subject involved and with the situation, in the majority of cases the attention span of a person is relatively short.

Most research into this aspect of communication has taken place with audience attention spans in presentations, but there is no reason to believe that the findings in this area differ widely from other communication situations. All indications are that a presentation, ie a talk or training course input session, is counterproductive if it extends beyond 20 minutes. Even this short period is reduced if the event is talk and chalk only – in these circumstances it appears that full attention starts to fall off rapidly after about ten minutes. This unhappy situation can, of course, be remedied. If visual aids are used during the talk the interest level is maintained for a longer period, because the monotonous feature of talk alone is interrupted – after each visual aid it is *almost* as if the talk is starting again. Attention is retained for an even longer period if other activities, such as buzz groups, experiential activities etc are introduced. The obvious messages, knowing what factors can extend the attention of an audience, are (1) keep the event as short as possible, (2) don't try to cram too much information into a short period, (3) support the talk with visual or audio-visual aids, (4) interrupt the talk flow at frequent intervals with active interventions. Even with these strategies a speaker should not expect complete attention, except perhaps at the start of the event and at the end when the audience knows that the presentation is coming to a close! This suggests that your most important points should be delivered at the beginning and, in a very impactive manner, at the end.

There is a close relationship between these approaches and more informal interactions and those with a smaller number of people, eg when a manager has to talk to a member of staff about the introduction of a new procedure. This must be performed in easy stages, using as many relevant visual images as possible to support the words; it should be an active interaction rather than the other person having to sit passively while the manager does all the talking; there should be plenty of opportunities for clarification and feedback, with interim and final summaries, and arrangements for review and control.

BLOCKS TO RECALL

The attention span is not the only problem with communication between people and trying to guarantee that the message is as effective as possible. Even though effective measures are taken to try to ensure maximum attention, there is no surety that the message, discussion or instruction will be remembered sufficiently to permit implementation. In the manager/staff example given above, although there is confirmation at the end of the interaction that everything has been said, heard and understood, introduction of the new procedure may not happen. The member of staff can easily forget a critical part of the procedure and so fail to implement it.

Again, most of the research into memory recall has related to the recall of the material presented in a talk or instructional session, and some studies have been so confined to pure research approaches that its application to 'real life' may not be completely relevant. However, unless we are blessed with an exceptional memory, a substantial amount of what we have heard, understood and immediately memorized will soon be forgotten – various factors of interest, age, length of time since the event, complexity, ease of remembering words as opposed to numbers etc can all affect the recall. In many cases the amount actually remembered after 24 hours is as little as 25 per cent! This is a salutary figure when we know we have planned, researched and designed an effective presentation, used the most effective ways of presenting, used summaries and so on with the intention that our 'audience' remembers most of what is said. The principal method of attempting to ensure a greater degree of recall is some form of repetition. The more usual opportunity for repetition occurs during a training course or similar interaction with the introduction of the same topic in different guises – the conscious may not immediately relate the similarities unless they are pointed out, but the subconscious will help this process. Longer-term 'repetition' can be aided by the recommendation to the other person to take notes, or in relevant cases to issue a handout. Recall is the one occasion when the written word becomes a very important vehicle, because reference back to grey or misunderstood areas becomes so much easier.

COMMUNICATION SKILL

The intention behind the introduction of the material to this point has been to demonstrate the problems of communication between people, and these help us to understand why interpersonal communication goes wrong on so many occasions – 'Weren't you listening when I told you?!', 'How could you forget that part of it?!' How often are comments such as these made to you? I would suggest that the response is likely to be 'Quite frequently!'

Of course, we can improve our communication skills to varying extents in several ways – reading about and understanding the problems and solutions, reflecting on the ways our communication interactions succeed or fail, seeking and accepting feedback from others about how they see our 'skills', attending training and development events to improve these skills. Once you have identified your existing level of skill you can move through the competence ladder (as shown in Figure 3.3) to increase your success in the events in which you have to communicate.

Unconscious incompetence. Many of us carry on our people interactions without considering how effective we really are, and we frequently wonder at a superficial level why they do not always work out as they should. There could be many reasons, of course, but a common one is that we are not very competent at people skills, but are unaware of this incompetence.

Conscious incompetence. Something may happen that lets us know that we are not as competent as we thought (or didn't think) we were. This might have been a serious self-inspection of our interactions and their results; or we may have received critical feedback about our skills in this area; or, for whatever reason, we attended a training event that

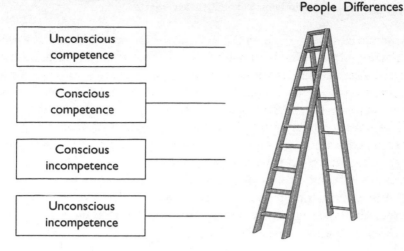

Figure 3.3 *The competence ladder*

helped us identify the level of our skills. As a result we move up the ladder to awareness of our incompetence.

Conscious competence. This comes about as a result of our actions to improve our skills and we start to practise, keeping in mind all the techniques and approaches we should be using. Practice is an important aspect of this stage, during which we are deliberately trying to improve.

Unconscious competence. The ultimate level is reached after considerable practice, both in a training situation and in real life, in which communication skills become second nature. The parallel is with learning to drive a car – during the learning stage we consciously think about changing gear, depressing pedals, steering as required and so on. After passing the test and developing experience through a significant amount of driving we begin to realize that we have changed gear, braked, corrected steering etc without thinking about what we were doing.

Remember that competence in communication is not only about ensuring that the actions *we* take are effective, the other person has their own levels, barriers, attitudes etc, and we may have to return to conscious competence to ensure that we are approaching that person in the most effective way. In order to do this, awareness and listening become very important aspects of communication.

LISTENING

This is a very specific skill, arguably the single most important aspect of communication. This must certainly be the case for the leading figure in an interactions, say the manager who has been asked to counsel a member of staff. In other interactions, for example a negotiation, it is essential that both sides listen carefully to what the others, including members of their own side, are saying. In a training or coaching event, although it might appear important that the learner concentrates on listening so that the skills in question can be absorbed, the trainer or coach must be listening even more intently to the learner so that reception and understanding signals can be picked up or messages heard that suggest an additional or alternative approach. However, many of us are very bad at listening; we are usually so keen to put in our own contribution that we just cannot wait for the other person to stop speaking. Consequently we are not listening to what they are saying, we simply know that they are speaking.

TRAPS TO LISTENING

Waiting to interrupt
Jumping to conclusions
Working out what you are going to say
Prejudices and judgmental views
Relating to your own experiences
Taking too much notice of lack of skills
Your own needs

Waiting to interrupt

This, as just mentioned, is probably the most common cause of not listening to the speaker. This trap suggests that the 'listener' feels that the speaker is saying something less important than what they want to say – commonly this happens when two people are talking to each other. Or the 'listener' is an enthusiast and simply cannot wait to make their contribution. Whatever the reason, and there are many others, interruption must be restrained. In an assertive situation, the thought to retain is that although 'I have a right to say what I want to say, the other person has an equal right'. Consequently, even though you are itching to interrupt, not only let the other person have their say, but *listen* to what they are saying. If you *must* interrupt, and this is valid on occasions, try to do this when the other is actually not speaking – they may have paused for breath, or may be collecting their thoughts before continuing. But you must be certain that your interruption is valid, otherwise wait until the other has stopped speaking.

Jumping to conclusions

Our listening span is usually so relatively short that, as with interrupting, we tend to cut short the contributions of others, unless we deliberately discipline ourselves. One of the common listening failings is the tendency part-way through the contribution of the other person to jump to conclusions about what they are saying and are going to say. Consequently we assume the remainder of their contribution and frequently then interrupt them with our response to the assumed comment. Two errors can occur as a result of this – first, we have ignored their rights and interrupted them and, second, we have said that we know what they are going to say. In the second case, they may not have said everything they wanted to say, and some of this may change the whole sense of their contribution, or, by interrupting, you might have misinterpreted what they were saying.

The correction of this error is simple in theory although, as with other people skills, not necessarily easy. This is to hold back and wait until the other's contribution is finished, listening carefully all the time and only reaching a conclusion when all the information has been given.

Working out what you are going to say

Conversations between two or more people involve, within limits, each participant taking turns at speaking. In theory while one person is talking the others are listening, then the next speaker enters the discussion. However, particularly if the subject being discussed is complex or very important, part of the listening time can be taken up with the 'listener' thinking about and working out what they are going to say when their 'turn' to speak arrives. Obviously, if this internal thinking process is going on, the person cannot be listening 100 per cent to the speaker, and in the worst scenario not listening at all. The result of this is that communication interaction is not taking place, rather there is a series of independent monologues, hopefully connected.

It is very difficult in certain circumstances to avoid this trap, but fortunately our brains are capable of performing two functions at the same time, although we must be careful not to permit the self-centred part to become dominant. It is simple to say, as some advisers do, that you should give complete attention to what the other is saying, then respond, but such a discussion would become very disjointed by the pauses, while each considers what response to give.

Prejudices and judgmental views

It has been commented that we all possess these to some extent and that they present a barrier to communication. We have to be careful when listening to the views of the other person to balance them in as neutral a way as possible. This is not easy, particularly if the subject conflicts with strong prejudices we hold, and however strong the arguments put forward by the speaker. But remember the inalienable rights of people to have views and put these forward, particularly if you have sought them. This is not to deny your own rights – however judgmental – but you must try to balance them with the strength of the arguments put forward.

Relating to your own experiences

Frequently when another person is talking with you they start describing a situation or event that rings bells with you as an experience you have had at some time in your life. Unless you are careful, rather than store this realization for *eventual* comment, you start thinking about the event rather than listening to the speaker. The effective action is, having made a mental note of the personal event (if it is indeed relevant) to continue listening to the speaker and, when it is your turn to talk, to use the event as part of your response.

Taking too much notice of lack of skills

Comments have been made earlier about language and its various facets acting as barriers, particularly between you and any listeners – jargon, words, accents etc. The reverse can apply equally when you are in the listening position. The various barriers may get in the way of your concentration and understanding, particularly if they are extreme, but a further factor may be introduced. The language barrier may be so evident that, instead of trying to come to terms with it, you allow it to intrude and you become frustrated with the speaker and the way they are expressing themselves, rather than with *what* they are saying.

Your own needs

In spite of all our decisions to overcome the various traps just described, we can be overcome by the very intrusive aspects described in the lower levels of Maslow's Hierarchy of Needs – our basic physical and mental needs. I can recall one occasion when I had to listen to an important statement made by one of my bosses. I missed some parts of it because my daughter had had an accident and was at that time undergoing an operation. My mind was on this rather than the current listening need. The effect was so significant that I had to stop my boss, tell him what was going on and that I just could not concentrate – fortunately he was a good boss and terminated the interaction in the best possible manner.

Illness – of self and others, house purchase and selling, death, imminent redundancy or promotion, imminent moves of location or job, are all basic aspects of our lives and can take precedence over what others are saying. If these are all-pervading and will seriously impinge on your listening, it is much better to declare them and make some other arrangements than try to compete with the other's comments.

If we consider the barriers and traps described in these two chapters on communication it will be realized that, although communication is the essential part of interpersonal interactions, many things can intervene to destroy it. If you are going into an important interaction it is essential that you bear in mind these barriers and traps and the ways to avoid them, rather than simply think – as so often happens – 'Oh, it'll be OK when we get going.' This thought is frequently the precursor to communication failure.

4

—

Communication and Behaviour

This chapter:

- discusses types of contributions to interactions
- describes aspects of personal presentation
- describes questioning skills and handling difficult replies.

EXPRESSING YOURSELF

Communication and people interaction are two-way processes in which both participants have to take an active part. The two previous chapters have concentrated on what you should be doing to ensure that you are giving the other person every opportunity to fulfil their part of the interaction. But you too must be playing an active and effective part – sometimes by doing or saying nothing. There will be parts of the interaction when you have to ensure that what you have to say is effective and stands every chance of being heard, listened to and understood by the other. All the barriers and traps discussed so far must be taken into account, but there are also other techniques that you can employ to try to ensure success.

YOUR CONTRIBUTIONS TO THE INTERACTION

The prime requirement for your contributions to any interaction in which you are involved is that they must be relevant. However, this alone is no guarantee that they will be listened to, let alone accepted. You must ensure that your contributions are as assertive as possible, otherwise you might as well not make them! A number of factors have to be taken into account in the range of possible interactions, and many of these depend on the type of event. For example, your status in the organization may have an effect on how you make your contributions; and the nature of the interaction will dictate the types of your contribution – counsellor, negotiator, disciplinarian, trainer or coach and so on. But there are several aspects that will be common to most, which include the following:

THE TYPE OF COMMUNICATION

A significant decision that you must make will depend on the nature of the communication and to what extent it has to be an interaction in every sense of the word between you and the others. The basic choice, which occurs more frequently than we imagine, is whether the communication should be one- or two-way.

One-way communication is still a common approach in organizations in spite of all the exhortations to make communication interactive. The more senior managers in an organization frequently practise one-way communication: a message has to be given, it is given, and then the speaker disappears, satisfied that the message has been given as instructed. You can easily imagine the problems that this approach encourages, and yet the practice still occurs.

The message is not fully understood
There are no opportunities to clarify
   misunderstandings
The content of the message is not accepted
Antagonism arises because of patronization
The instruction fails to be implemented
At worst, the message results in
   industrial action

Situations in which this one-way communication occurs, rightly or wrongly, include:

Lectures on training courses
Formal addresses by senior management
Exhortations at annual conferences
Secondary messages by junior managers
   originating 'upstairs'
Videoed messages shown throughout
the organization

The reason for communication of this nature, often fondly believed by the speaker to be interaction with the audience, is the mistaken belief within an organization that it is the quickest and most efficient method. If the message is clear then it is a speedy method of communicating, but it can obviously initiate many of the problems detailed above. If the message has been inefficiently prepared and/or presented almost complete failure results. There may be times when you are put into this position with no opportunity to present in a more humane manner. In such circumstances you should ensure that the form of the message is as simple, as unambiguous and as clear as you make it, so at least many of the misunderstandings and some of the non-acceptances can be resolved or modified.

Whatever the attitude of the organization, if you are the manager of the group of people to whom you have had to deliver the one-way message you are courting failure or even disaster if you do not follow up the message with some action. Sub-meetings can be held to respond to questions from the staff or, if this is not allowed, personal and individual contacts can be made to obtain feedback and resolve problems. It must be borne in mind that one-way 'interactions' of this kind rarely succeed, the only 'benefit' is that minimum time is expended – *at the time*.

Contrary approaches are based on two-way communication, and these offer the greatest opportunity for success in an interaction. The basis for this statement returns us to the aspect of assertiveness and the rights of both sides in an interaction. It is your right to present the message with the intention that it is understood and accepted, and it is the listeners' right to have their needs listened to and as far as possible accepted, and to make contributions in response to the message. Immediate feedback and clarification are possible, which aids acceptance and certainly encourages the attitudes of the listeners. There can obviously be no guarantee that the listeners will leave the meeting fully motivated, with complete understanding and without disagreement or frustration, but at least the opportunity will have been given to them to air their views and questions *at the time*. The wise manager will follow this meeting up, as with the one-way situation, with efforts to obtain feedback. The negative aspects of this format will principally be its time-consuming nature, particularly where the subject is complex and substantial clarification is necessary. The speaker must also be as experienced and skilled as possible to avoid all the traps we have seen – this is often the reason why uncertain speakers revert to the one-way approach.

MAKING YOUR CASE

As with most cases in presenting information or having a people inter-action, much will depend on the situation and various aspects that relate to this, but I can commend a general approach that will serve many situations and can easily be modified. The approach is simple and straightforward and can be summarized as follows.

1. State your information, view or proposition
2. Show evidence and proof to support this, including counters to opposition arguments that you have already anticipated
3. Repeat the information, view or proposition in a summarized form
4. Seek questions, views, agreement etc from the audience
5. Review the discussion and summarize the results
6. Review the presentation and summarize the key points.

Notice that, as suggested earlier, repetition – in this case in the form of summaries – forms a significant part of the message presentation and time is included for the two-way aspect of the event.

PERSONAL PRESENTATION

Effective methods of presenting yourself are numerous and need another text to record them fully, but three useful techniques are worth mentioning here – the four Ps, MERK and KISS.

The four Ps

The four Ps relate to the way you can use your voice to greatest effect, particularly when you are speaking to a group of people.

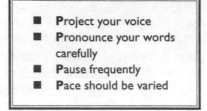

- **P**roject your voice
- **P**ronounce your words carefully
- **P**ause frequently
- **P**ace should be varied

Projection is important, particularly when you are not used to speaking to a group and/or not used to speaking in rooms larger than your own. It will be of little use if you have some wonderful material and messages if the people at the rear of the group cannot hear you. So you will need to throw your voice to the back of the room. Try this out with a colleague have your colleague sit at the back of the room and try speaking with different volumes until the most appropriate one is obvious. However, with your audience present, there will be coughs, breathing, moving or creaking chairs, so it will be necessary to raise the volume a step or so from the one you found in the rehearsal.

Pronunciation. Have you a regional accent? Does it matter? Is the audience from your region? With a more national audience, would your accent interfere with their understanding? You may have to try to modify your accent, but do not be ashamed of it, particularly if it is attractive. The caveat must be that it can be understood by people who are not familiar with it, which is frequently not the case with a strong regional accent for people from other parts of Britain.

Words, particularly their endings, are easily lost in a largish audience – so pronounce your words slightly more precisely than you do in normal conversation. But make sure that this does not sound artificial.

Are you likely to use any difficult words, particularly any with which you have had problems in the past? Check their pronunciation and rehearse this until it ceases to be a problem, or find a different word to use.

Because you are talking to a larger group of people than normal, and because words can be lost in such situations, tend to overemphasize your words and, in complex, multi-syllable words, accentuate the syllables so that the whole word is clear.

Pause frequently so that both you and the audience can catch up with what has been said. Pauses can also be used for effect – a pause (say for a silent count of four) before an important word or statement can alert the audience to the fact that something they should listen to is coming. Don't be worried by silences – they will seem longer to you than to your audience.

Pace. This should be varied, not only to break the monotony of a single-pace speech, but also for effect. Increasing the speed of delivery can suggest importance or excitement and the audience can be stimulated to increase their reception speed. Slow the delivery down and the words become more dramatic and again demonstrate importance. The tone and pitch of your voice should also be varied for interest and impact, and repetition of key words or phrases in a different tone, at a different speed, or with different emphases will also draw attention to these points.

As mentioned earlier, you should aim to talk at a rather slower speed than normal, particularly if you are a normally rapid talker. It may sound to you that you are speaking too slowly, but it will not do so to the listeners, who are being given the opportunity of hearing your words rather than having to race their minds to keep up with you. However, don't overdo this, as too slow a pace might suggest a lack of enthusiasm on your part and a resultant drop in their enthusiasm.

MERK

Another technique that is useful in controlling your voice when addressing groups of people is MERK, a mnemonic helping you to remember to:

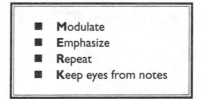

> ■ **M**odulate
> ■ **E**mphasize
> ■ **R**epeat
> ■ **K**eep eyes from notes

Modulate the tone of your voice to keep it interesting – use drama, apparent monotony, harshness, softness and so on.
Emphasize certain parts of the speech for effect.
Repeat key words and phrases to emphasize their importance and ensure understanding and recall.

Keep your eyes away from your notes except at necessary intervals. Otherwise your volume will drop, you may seem to mumble and your credibility will be reduced if it appears that you are simply reading from a script.

KISS

KISS is a mnemonic for what is often considered to be the most important advice to people who have to speak to others, whether this is to a single person, a small number of people, or a large group. KISS is summarized as:

KEEP
IT
SHORT
and
SIMPLE

KISS, which is sometimes varied to read 'Keep it simple, stupid!', embodies many of the aspects of advice so far suggested. The shorter you make your contribution, while ensuring that you give sufficient detail to make the initial impact, the more likely is it that the listeners will listen to all your message. Keeping it simple helps to ensure understanding and will reduce the number of questions needed for clarification. You are also obviously neither patronizing the listeners with over-simplicity nor using simplicity to hide complexity or induce misunderstanding.

QUESTIONING SKILLS

Much of the communication behaviour of the interactions initiator (eg the manager interviewing a member of staff) will consist of questioning the other person. The success or otherwise of the interaction may rely on the skill of the questioner, and this is a further skill that people interactors must learn. Remember that a question only deserves a response at the level at which it is posed – ask a silly question and you should expect a silly answer!

If you intend to ask questions of the other person at any time during the interaction it helps considerably if, as far as possible, these questions, or at least the types of questions, are prepared in advance.

Questions can be posed in a variety of ways (examples are given below), and in many cases the response is based on the format of the question. When you ask a question you should know *why* you are asking that form of question and what sort of response you are likely to receive.

Closed questions. These normally require (and obtain) a simple answer 'yes' or 'no' answer or a straightforward statement of facts. For example, 'Have you ever conducted an appraisal interview?' or 'Who was your last employer?'. Closed questions usually require another question to be asked immediately, unless you have elicited all the information you require.

Presumptive questions. These are usually closed questions that assume part of the answer. For example (without any previous information), 'What sort of car do you drive?' This assumes that the other person has a car and that they can drive.

Leading questions. These tend to be negatively presumptive questions that obviously suggest the questioner is expecting a certain answer. This may put the other person on the spot, depending on their relationship with the questioner. An example of a leading question is 'I expect you will want to start your appraisal interview programme without any further training or delay?'

Multiple questions. These are in fact a series of questions strung together. They can cause problems for the responder, who may not remember all the parts of the question and consequently (or sometimes deliberately) answer one part only – usually the last part: 'Have you got a driving licence, when did you get it and what groups is it for? Where did you take your test? Can you drive a range of vehicles?'

Rambling questions. Similar to the multiple question but without the specifically identifiable parts of that type of question. The rambling question goes on and on until the listener is unsure what is being asked.

Conflict questions. These are designed to produce a reaction from the other person and may (whether or not this is intended) produce a negative or emotional response. If an emotional response does not emerge it may be that they are being suppressed, eg 'I might have expected you to react like that, mightn't I?'

Hypothetical questions. Usually intended to test a responder's problem-solving ability by posing a hypothetical situation, such as 'If you were given an unlimited budget to set up a learning resource centre, how would you go about this?'. This type of question can test ability and knowledge but, being hypothetical, may receive only a hypothetical response.

Open questions. Usually begin with *What, How, Why* and, less openly, *Who, Where* and *When*. They are used to open up the discussion as the response is less likely to be monosyllabic, eg 'How would you describe an appraisal interview?'

They can also be an invitation to give extended information, as in 'Tell me about some of the experiences you have had in the appraisal interviews you have conducted.'

Probing questions. These are open questions which seek further or clarified information on responses already given, eg 'You said you had done so and so. Can you tell me more about that work?' The presenter should be prepared to ask such an 'instant' type of question, particularly if the responder(s) to the original question have been vague, evasive or have given incomplete answers.

Testing understanding. A variation on the probing question that sets out to ensure that the questioner has put over a point correctly, the other person has understood what the questioner has asked or said, or the questioner has understood what the responder has said. For example, 'If I've got it right you are suggesting that. . . Is that right?'

Reflection. This is not really a question, but its basic intention is to encourage the responder to give more information without having to be asked a question directly. If the other person has made a brief comment such as, 'I'm having some problems with the new procedure', but appears unwilling to extend this information, a reflection might be 'It seems that the problem is mainly with the new procedure.' Hopefully, the other person will then say 'Yes, that's right. What I am being asked to do is. . .'

One word of caution about questioning. Because of the variety of people and their personalities, responses as suggested above cannot be guaranteed, and you must be prepared for answers that do not follow the 'rules'.

HANDLING DIFFICULT REPLIES

If you ask a question you expect a response and, if you have posed the question in the most effective manner, you will receive a response more or less in the form you anticipated or hoped for. But not all responses will fall into these categories and you must be prepared to deal with them effectively. Often, when planning the questions you will ask, it is possible to identify the occasions when the responses may be other than those desired. These might include:

When the answer is incorrect or incomplete. Do not ridicule, be sarcastic or ignore it. Show appreciation for a response and acknowledge any incomplete part that is correct. Then pass to the remainder and either correct it or, preferably, probe the responder for the correct answer.

When the answer is woolly but the responder obviously had the correct answer in mind. Comment that you have some idea of what the responder is saying, but you would benefit from clarification (select the woolliest parts for this).

When the question is received with silence. Ask yourself 'Was the question clear?' Had you over-estimated the person's ability? Break the question into smaller steps. The silence may be accompanied by puzzled looks – this will indicate to you non-verbally that the person has not understood, rather than their having some other reason for not responding.

When the response asks for your views. This is a ploy people often use either to put you on the spot or to avoid having to commit themselves. State openly in response that you know (or don't know) the answer, but you would prefer them to provide the information.

VIEWPOINTS

Any interaction, even one of the same type, can be approached in different ways, according to the viewpoint of the various individuals. Imagine a group of people standing at the summit of a mountain and looking down into the valleys below. The people in the group will be having different thoughts about how they see this view, depending on their viewpoints on life – these can be identified from their physical and verbal reactions.

Figure 4.1 suggests the internal dialogues these observers will be experiencing, representing the various viewpoints that can be taken. For example B, who thinks 'Looking all the way around and down, isn't it all wonderful', is taking the global view and in other situations may be uncomfortable if forced to look at specifics before they are ready. Interactions with this type of person may need a long introductory period before settling down to the point. However if that 'slowly, slowly' approach is taken with A, who is thinking 'Well, I've reached the top; let's go and do something else', the result may be failure. In such a case 'Good morning. Let's get down to business' may be more effective.

This is one of the most difficult aspects of people interactions. If the initiator does not know the other people and their viewpoints well, an assessment has to be made early in the interaction based on limited knowledge, a risky situation.

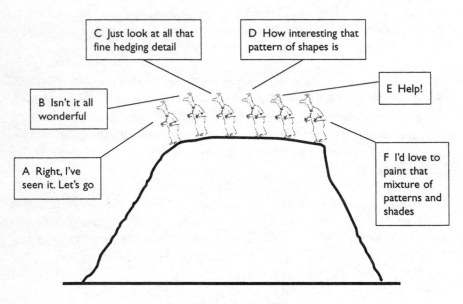

Figure 4.1 *Viewpoints*

5
—

Observing Behaviour

This chapter:

- describes some models of human behaviour
- describes the practice of behaviour analysis in the observation of groups.

MODELS OF HUMAN BEHAVIOUR

The investigation of human behaviour is the principal aspect of psychology and the many models used in training are psychology based. Unless you are a psychologist-trainer you must be very careful not to become or try to think as an amateur psychologist – in dealing with people skills you are dealing with the internal functions of people, and untrained practitioners usually do much more harm than good. This is where the difference between personality and behaviour is important – the personality, normal or abnormal – is the realm of the psychologist and psychiatrist, whereas behaviour is the overt exhibition of this personality, real or modified, and is the realm in which the trainer operates. The line between personality and behaviour is very thin and the trainer should be careful not to stray too far. However, if the people skills trainer is to be effective, these psychology-based models must be the basis of the training, always with the caveat that they should be used with care.

Although using training approaches based on sound psychological research, observation and models, the training practitioner must:

Avoid trying to ape the professionally trained psychologist
Avoid the temptation to behave as an amateur psychologist
Avoid the use of the word psychology (frequently a turn-off
    for lay people)
Use words that the people can understand

Psychological models related to training and people skills are constantly appearing (and disappearing), many of them flavours of the month, but a number of well-established ones have stood the test of time and are readily acceptable by the majority of learners. These models include:

Maslow's Hierarchy of Needs
The Herzberg Approach
The Managerial Grid
The Johari Window
Behaviour Analysis

MASLOW'S HIERARCHY OF NEEDS

This hierarchy can have important implications for the trainer who is trying to encourage a learner or group of learners to apply themselves fully to the learning opportunities. This does not always happen, and in many cases the position of the learner in the hierarchy is responsible. This hierarchy was produced by Abraham Maslow, who saw that human needs could be identified as being at different levels, the lower levels of which must be satisfied to some extent before the individual can consider the higher levels. The hierarchy is illustrated in Figure 5.1. The needs are intrinsic to human nature and at the lowest level represent the need to survive physically and physiologically – the requirement for air, food, water and sleep. These are essential for life and must be present before the next level – that of the more long-term survival factors – shelter, clothing, a job, job security and so on. These appear basic to all of us, but without these survival factors the individual has no motivation to try to move further up the hierarchy and little that anyone can do will produce movement.

When the two lower levels of basic physical needs are satisfied the scene is set to allow deeper desires to surface and involve the more

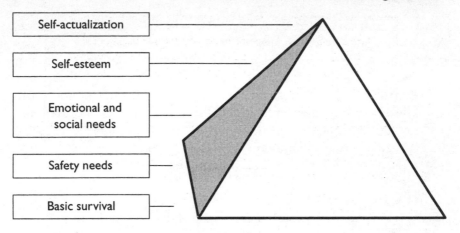

Figure 5.1 *Maslow's Hierarchy of Needs*

emotional needs. Such factors as belonging (to society, to a group, to a family), friendship and affection, and embracing the involvement of other people will normally be the next satisfactions for humans to aim at. Of course, there are individuals to whom these needs appear to mean nothing – the loner, the hermit, the recluse – but even to them belonging is part of their existence: would the loner be content if no other people existed?!

At a deeper psychological level is the next stage of the hierarchy that involves the need for an individual's esteem, in terms of both self-respect and the respect of others, competence, independence, self-confidence and prestige. The person's attitudes and motivation to perform, including learning, interacting with others and behaving in an appropriate way with others have now reached an outward-looking concept of life, rather than the egocentric, inward-looking attitude that restrains upward movement.

Once this important level is attained and the individuals are in effect at peace with themselves the aim can be self-actualization, in which self-fulfilment in the widest way, real self-expression and creativity can be achieved. The individual's work may or may not offer these outlets, but if not they will be sought away from work. Painters, writers, sculptors, top sportspeople and entrepreneurs have achieved this level, often moving to these expressive areas from more mundane jobs where the earlier hierarchical needs can be achieved. Self-actualization is self-perpetuating and produces a dissatisfaction with successive achievement. The artist who has produced a painting strives to produce a better one; the writer who has created a literary work will not rest until an even better work has been completed; the entrepreneurial businessman who has built up a successful enterprise will then seek other avenues for business success, often without the desire to make even more money.

Maslow suggests that human behaviour will be motivated only by an unsatisfied need at any of the levels. The choice of levels is not necessarily from lower to higher, and skipping of levels often occurs. Circumstances and pressures, social, economic, mental etc, will also have an effect. The practical aspect of the model is that there is little point in attempting to motivate someone to achieve a particular level when the level at which they find themselves has not been successfully conquered.

In the area of people skills that we are considering the hierarchical levels are in many ways skill levels themselves, and in the upper areas the good people interactor will try to become even more effective.

THE HERZBERG APPROACH

The powerful and widely recognized model of Frederick Herzberg is, like Maslow, based on needs, but Herzberg concentrates on two types of basic needs – the maintenance or hygiene factor and the motivational need.

The hygiene factors relate to Maslow's lower levels and are concerned with people's material needs, but Herzberg's point is that, once these are satisfied, they become not only cyclical but often progressive. Cyclically, if I breathe, I have to breathe again; if I eat I have to eat again. However, if one year I am give a pay rise I expect a pay rise again next year, but I expect it to be larger. If my manager does something for me I am grateful, but soon want something else – the 'What have you done for me lately?' syndrome. Herzberg contends that to satisfy and motivate people the hygiene factors must be fulfilled, but this does not work as often as it is attempted.

In trying to deal effectively with people, to motivate them and to encourage them to do their best and to do what you want them to do, in addition to the satisfaction of the hygiene factors the motivational needs of most people must also be satisfied. The motivational satisfactions that can encourage people are concerned with their needs for personal growth, achievement, responsibility and recognition. These can be achieved at work through job satisfaction, job enrichment and enlargement, more control over what is done, and the opportunity to expand skills and knowledge.

It is obviously important to keep these needs in mind when developing people skills and using them in real-life situations.

THE MANAGERIAL GRID

This model for considering people and their needs stems from Robert Blake and Jane Mouton and identifies the attitudes of people by their concerns – concerns for people against their concern for production achievement. Managers must relate these two concerns when deciding on the most effective style to maintain effective staff and achieve the organizational aims.

Figure 5.2 summarizes in graphic form the managerial concerns for people against production or task.

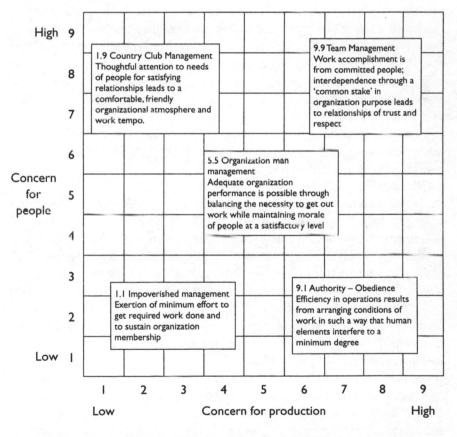

Figure 5.2 *The Managerial Grid*

(From Robert R Blake and Jane S Mouton (1978) *The New Managerial Grid*, Gulf Publishing Co, Houston.)

A 1.1 manager has a low concern for both people and production and consequently makes no effort to become committed, neither straining to excel in producing nor building good relationships with their staff. They are usually non-directive people who will not take sides in a disagreement, not because a neutral stance is preferred, but because they do not want to become involved in conflict. These attitudes do not encourage loyalty and although the staff do not know where the managers stand, they do not care. In specific interactions staff are unlikely to take much notice of any managerial comments or advice.

On the other hand 1.9 managers go out of their way to have warm, friendly relationships with their staff and other people, and defer to this at the expense of the task. Conflict is something to be avoided at all costs, but if it cannot be avoided the manager will try to soothe the bad feelings generated. When staff do not behave as 1.9 managers would wish, they feel they have failed and need to do something to restore the warm feelings needed. If people realize these attitudes (and they generally do), although they are friendly to the manager they are suspicious of the basis of any advice given.

Diametrically opposite to the 1.9 style is the 9.1 style, in which the emphasis is on production and the task rather than people. Tight control is maintained and the task achievement reduces people concern to a minimum; obedience to their managers' authority is demanded and they will press their own views and ideas even if this generates conflict, which will be ignored or stamped out.

Management at the 5.5 level at first sight appears to be an ideal situation, in which the managers try to balance production output with a satisfactory people relationship, accomplished by compromise and a reliance on systems and tradition. They rarely take the initiative, preferring others to take the lead or find a safe approach; they will then go along with this view so that popularity can be maintained.

The 9.9 style is characterized by commitment to high task achievement, but not at the expense of the people concerned. The 9.9 manager succeeds through consultation, participation, involvement and the development of people commitment. The manager works hard to develop teams, not to control them, but for them to produce constructive ideas for which they will be empowered to ownership. If the views of other people are sounder the 9.9 manager will be willing to change his or her view, and conflict is treated as a natural event, brought into the open and resolved and used as a learning process. In this atmosphere people relationships are good and interactions proceed effectively as normal events, everybody understanding and appreciating the views, ideas, advice and guidance of others.

THE JOHARI WINDOW

The Johari Window model is similar to the Managerial Grid in application to people skills, but in this case the concentration of attention is on the personal and internal aspects of people and their observed behaviour.

The model originated with Joseph Luft and Harry Ingram – hence the title which is composed from their forenames, Jo + Hari(y). The model raises the concept that there is a four-paned window that can be seen through to show or reflect the various aspects of our behaviour. If these aspects can be recognized we can adjust our dealings with people accordingly, or, in a training environment, awareness can be increased to enable people to modify their behaviour. The window is two-way, with information flowing out from people and feedback from others entering that person's window.

The window has four panes, shown in Figure 5.3, each pane representing knowledge at the various levels. The panes will not be equal sizes from one individual to another, and each individual's window is capable of modification, either as an increase of trust between people or as a result of accepted feedback interchanged between individuals.

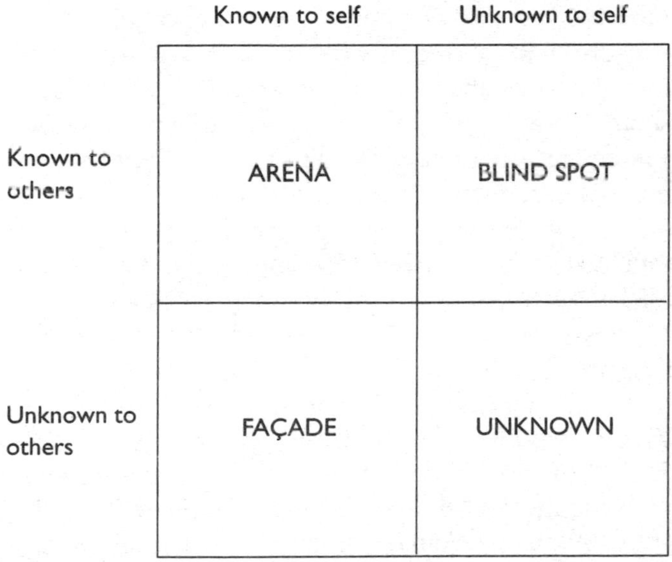

	Known to self	Unknown to self
Known to others	ARENA	BLIND SPOT
Unknown to others	FAÇADE	UNKNOWN

Figure 5.3 *The Johari Window*

The top left pane is entitled the Arena and represents what we know about ourselves that is also known by others – the area of open and public knowledge. The size of this pane can vary considerably according to the openness of the individuals and their willingness to expose information about themselves. The pane is very much under the control of the person, and even with feedback the overt image is determined completely by that person.

Another pane, related to the Arena and capable of modification in a similar way, is the Façade or Hidden area. This section of the awareness model is concerned with things that are known about oneself, like the Arena, but unknown to others. The Façade is clearly related to the various public acts or roles we perform, roles we want other people to consider as the real us.

The ability we have to act out roles determines whether the Façade is maintained or whether our act is discerned and the pane is transferred into the Arena. Many people maintain a Façade because of a false sense of security, because of being very 'private', or at worst to mislead others for some nefarious purpose. Other individuals may be afraid that, if they reveal their true selves, they will suffer emotionally.

The third pane, the Blind Spot, represents the area about us of which we are unaware, but which is observable to others. This pane can be reduced and our awareness of ourselves increased as a result of the increase in trust between ourselves and others. In such cases feedback can be given and accepted and behaviour modification considered. The more the feedback the greater the reduction possible in the Blind Spot.

The final window pane is the most difficult one as far as awareness and behaviour movement is concerned, for this is the Unknown area which contains information about us of which neither ourselves nor others are aware. Some of these aspects about ourselves may be so deeply hidden that they never surface, but others may be lurking just underneath the psychological surface, and with the right stimulus may come to light. Such Unknown aspects may be skills that have never emerged, or may require significant pressure, trauma or solicitation to bring them out.

The format of an individual's window can determine their skills in their interactions with others, and the awareness skills of others will enable them to assess people with whom they come into contact. It is obviously difficult to assess the values of somebody's window in a short period of time, particularly if they have a strong Façade and are skilled at protecting this; the longer the interaction the more change can occur in the window, with consequent help in improving interaction. The Façade will rarely completely disappear since few of us will divulge everything about ourselves to everybody, but posturing can be reduced when trust increases. If all the three active panes of the window that can be affected – Arena, Façade and Blind Spot – are reduced to a realistic minimum there is every chance that the Unknown area will be reduced, with other skills coming to light.

Certain individuals are the most difficult to identify. One such has a small Arena and a large Façade. These are usually shy or very quiet people with whom it is difficult to have an interaction. Little movement will occur and interactions will continue to be difficult if their window is not modified. One result of their Johari profile is that they will almost certainly have a large Blind Spot, because they are not given or do not accept feedback, and a large Unknown area, as this is not encouraged to open up. These people will rarely seek help and, in a more formal interaction, the leading person will have difficulties communicating with them and assessing not only where the problems lie but whether the advice or support offered is being accepted.

BEHAVIOUR ANALYSIS

If I had to choose one people model that offers the most help in improving people skills it would be Behaviour Analysis, a firmly behaviour-anchored approach to identifying what is happening, and offering people an avenue to modify their behaviour following this awareness.

The basis for behaviour or interaction analyses rests largely in the observational instruments suggested by R F Bales and J Klein. These were principally research approaches and were too complex and difficult to use in people skill training events. Neil Rackham, Peter Honey and their associates found problems in people evaluation and assessment in what was then (1971) the British Overseas Airways Corporation (now British Airways). What emerged from their work in this area was an analytical instrument that had to satisfy a number of criteria before being found acceptable. Five of their criteria still stand before an analytical instrument can be accepted.

1.	Possibility for change
2.	Meaningfulness
3.	Reliability
4.	Degree of differentiation
5.	Relationship to outcome

1. *Possibility for change.* It is very interesting when observing people to observe *every* behaviour, whatever and how many there may be. But when we are considering people skills, training for these and modifying any that may need it, there is little point in observing and recording behaviours that cannot be changed or modified by the person displaying them.

2. *Meaningfulness.* The category of behaviour described must be understood by both the person exhibiting the behaviour and the person observing it. If observers do not understand it they will have difficulty in observing and identifying it and subsequently discussing it with the person concerned. If the person being observed does not understand it it will be rejected in feedback and the reasons for observing, analyzing and giving feedback will be undermined.

3. *Reliability.* When two or more observers watch an interaction there must be a statistically significant correlation between their results – numbers of contributions recorded, the behaviours themselves and the distribution of these categories throughout the interaction.

4. *Degree of differentiation.* This links strongly with the reliability criterion and requires the categories of behaviour to be sufficiently distinct from each other so that any confusion is kept to a minimum. One problem is that although a clear-cut category can be defined by the observer the actual behaviour of people is not equally clear and concise. Many contributions of verbal behaviour are made in a manner so woolly and obtuse that the listener has considerable difficulty in identifying what is being said. In such cases clearly distinguishable categories can help an interaction observation, but they do not produce the absolute answer.

5. *Relationship to outcome.* This is particularly important in a people skills training situation in which the behaviour must be relevant and applicable. In any interaction there will be behaviours that will be important to the outcome, just as there will be behaviours that will have little or no effect on the outcome. Observing the latter will obviously be a wasted effort.

Behaviour categories

Using these criteria Rackham and Honey produced a set of 13 categories that formed the basis of an analytical instrument for the observation of people in groups. This was entitled 'Behaviour Analysis' or BA. Eventual use of BA shows that an observer is not restricted to these categories, provided the five criteria are followed. The categories to be used depend on the type of event being observed.

The thirteen categories in the general purpose BA are as follows:

Proposing	Testing understanding
Building	Summarizing
Supporting	Seeking information
Disagreeing	Giving information
Defending/Attacking	Bringing in
Blocking/Difficulty stating	Shutting out
Open	

In behavioural terms, these categories describe:

Proposing. A behaviour that puts forward an idea or suggestion for a new course of action, frequently signalled by 'I propose that. . .', but more commonly as 'I think we should. . .', 'Let's. . .' or 'I suggest that we. . .'

Building. This is a proposal that extends or develops one that has been made by another person to enhance, not replace the original proposal. For example, if the first proposal suggests 'Let's go to the pictures tonight', a build could be 'Yes, we should go to the Odeon as there's a western on there and we all like westerns.' More than one build is possible, eg 'And then we could go for a Chinese meal.'

Supporting. This is a conscious or direct declaration of support for another person or their views. This can take the simple form of 'Yes, I agree' or 'Yes, I support (go along with) that', or it may be a longer contribution, saying the same as the original statement but using different words.

Disagreeing. The opposite behaviour to supporting, in which there is definite disagreement with the concepts or views of another, even the simple 'No, I don't agree (go along with) that'.

Defending/Attacking. These behaviours occur in a verbal conflict situation when one person speaks against another's views, the statement being delivered with emotive words, phrases or tones of expression. The statement 'I might have expected *you* to say that' can only be taken as an attack on the other's manner and approach. An attacking or defending statement will probably result, an ascending attack/defend spiral continuing until one of the individuals backs down or the 'fight' is stopped by a chairperson.

Blocking/Difficulty stating. This is a range of behaviours that add nothing nor help along the activity. A typical 'block' is 'We're just going around in circles', which usually stops the discussion dead until someone has to make a positive and constructive contribution for progress – 'Yes, we are, so let's summarize where we've got to.' The 'blocker' could easily have also said this, making the contribution positive rather than negative.

Facetious or 'funny' remarks are included in this category, depending on the scale and degree of their use. The occasional humorous remark can defuse a situation, but repeated comic remarks can soon give rise to antagonism.

Open. This is when a speaker admits an error or omission or apologizes for their actions. This type of contribution can range from the simple 'Sorry' to something like 'Yes, I'm afraid it's all my fault – I should have seen that reference in the report.' These apologies need not be negative, as they can sometimes be used to stop an attack/defend spiral, when one of the people involved realizes the futility of this and apologizes (whether or not they were to blame) to progress the event.

Testing understanding. This very useful behaviour can serve several purposes. A typical testing understanding statement starts with 'From what you have been saying, if I've got it right, you are suggesting. . .'. This contribution:

- allows the speaker to check their understanding of what was said
- gives others in a group the opportunity to check that *they* have also understood
- checks with the original contributor that they said what they meant to say and allows corrections to be made or omissions rectified.

Summarizing. This is very similar to testing understanding, but with specific checking back. The summary is a compact statement that collects the content of the discussion to that stage or from a previous event. The criteria are that it should be short and clear, but also correct and comprehensive.

Seeking information. These are contributions in which questions are asked about people's information, views, feelings, ideas, opinions and thoughts.

Giving information. The stating behaviour in which information, views, feelings, ideas, opinions and thoughts are given.

Bringing in. This is a gatekeeping category of behaviour, in which a specific person is asked to make a contribution. It usually includes the name of that person, for example, 'What do you think, George?' is seeking information that also specifically invites George to comment.

Shutting out. When one person interrupts another they are shutting them out of the interaction by:

- interrupting them before they have finished speaking
- participating in side conversations during a group discussion
- giving a view before that of a person who has been specifically brought in.

In each of these cases the interrupter(s) is saying 'I have something to say that is more important than your views!'

Using Behaviour Analysis

When BA is used to observe, the categories are entered on a BA form with spaces for markings to be made against these categories and for the person making them. In a group event, as it progresses, each speaker and the contribution they have made is identified in a category (note that the contribution is 'identified' not 'interpreted') and entered as a stroke on the form. This process continues for every contribution made. The end result of strokes on the form identifies:

- how many contributions in total were made by the group as a whole
- how many contributions in total were made by each person
- the categorization of each individual's contributions
- the categorization of the group's contributions.

Completion of the BA form is simple, with perhaps only three aspects requiring comment.

1. Each time a person speaks a stroke is entered in the box produced by the cross-reference to their name and the category. To make the record clearer and analysis simpler, five strokes can be made into the well-known five-bar gate – ⊞.

2. Normally there is only one stroke made each time a person speaks, usually for the most important or significant part of what they have said. This avoids the number of strokes for a long contribution getting out of hand. There will, however, be occasions when all parts of a contribution appear to have similar importance or weighting – this may mean that more than one stroke is necessary.

3. Bringing in and shutting out are normally the two exceptions to the single stroke 'rule'. Bringing in usually involves a question being asked of a named person: two strokes should be entered, one for the bringing in and the other for another category, usually a question. Similarly, shutting out requires two strokes – one for the shutting out and the other for the category contribution used in the shutting out.

An example of a BA form that can be used to record a group discussion including four people is shown in Figure 5.4.

Modifications of BA

One of the major advantages of BA as an observation and analysis instrument is its flexibility and the lack of constraints on the categories that can be used. Some of the modifications I have introduced in my use of BA with group observation include the categories of:

- Disagreeing
- Proposing
- Seeking ideas

and I use a BA with 16 categories in these situations.

Disagreeing

In the original category list of Rackham and Honey, disagreeing is shown as one category. I believe that disagreement can be both positive and negative. In the negative case, if someone simply disagrees without giving any reasons (as is frequently the case), I see this as a negative and unhelpful behaviour which should be identified as such. However, if there is disagreement it should certainly be stated, the person disagreeing should be positive and helpful and not only disagree but also state the reasons for their attitude. The latter approach certainly helps to avoid conflict situations. Consequently, I use two categories:

NAME: W L Rae   ACTIVITY: Discussion 1600h to 1635h

	BRIAN	MARY	RALPH	MICHAEL	TOTALS
PROPOSING		12	4	15	31
BUILDING		3			3
SEEKING IDEAS, INFORMATION	1	16	19	6	42
GIVING VIEWS, INFORMATION	12	14	25	22	73
SUMMARIZING		1			1
SUPPORTING	8	4	6	1	19
OPEN			2	1	3
DISAGREEING		2	1	6	9
ATTACKING BLOCKING DIFFICULTY STATING		6	6	8	20
BRINGING IN		2	1		3
SHUTTING OUT	1	8	14	15	38
TOTALS	22	68	78	74	242

Figure 5.4   *Behaviour Analysis form*

1. Disagreeing (that is, without reasons being given)
2. Disagreeing with reasons.

Proposing

Proposals for action can be made in several ways, two approaches being the most common:

1. Direct statement proposals – (the basic proposal behaviour as defined by Rackham) 'I propose that ...'; 'Let's...'; 'I think we should ...'
2. Suggestive proposals.

Research by Peter Honey showed that in many cases there was resistance to proposals made in the first way, people tending to think that something was being forced upon them, particularly if the proposer was a strong character. However, if the proposal is made in such a way that the others are given the opportunity, and in fact encouraged to have some ownership of the proposal, there is a greater likelihood of it being accepted – 42 per cent compared with 25 per cent. The suggestive proposal is put in the form of a question, although giving others something to consider – eg 'How would you feel if we. . .?' or 'What do you think about the idea that we might. . .?'

Seeking ideas

The original category was described as 'seeking information' and was a cover-all category for asking questions. But there is a significant difference between asking for information, views, opinions and feelings and seeking the presentation of ideas or proposals. Consequently I separated this category into two; the one following the original format of general seeking, the other specifically asking for ideas.

Obviously other categories could be added, but there is a distinct barrier to the number of categories included. The more categories the better defined are the behaviours, but the more difficult it becomes for the observer to identify and mark up the contributions. Most people, with a reasonable amount of training, are capable of coping with BA of about 11 categories. A different difficulty experienced by observers new to BA concerns the number of people in the group being observed. With experience, and following training, an observer should be able to cope well with 11 categories and a group of six. With groups larger than six the difficulties increase, although not proportionally. After all, even in a group of 20, only one person is speaking at a time *most* of the time. The real problems occur in the larger groups when the activity rate becomes high, a number of people speaking at the same time in quick succession, often with a high shutting-out rate. However, as we shall see in the next chapter, quite different conditions apply when we are using BA to observe situations different from those of the group.

Simpler forms of BA

The reverse position to increasing the number of BA categories in an attempt to make the results more comprehensive is to reduce the number, which especially makes it easier for BA beginners to use. Limited BAs can also be used on training events by observers who do not need to know the full extent of BA, or by those who may need to use BA on one or two occasions only – an example of this is in 'fishbowl' observation (see the following chapter).

Obviously a limited-category BA has a much more limited use than the 13 or 16 category example, but an optimum number of categories can be used to give useful feedback. The usual use for a limited BA is to demonstrate the variations between positive (helpful) and negative (unhelpful) behaviour. For this purpose, many untrained observers can cope satisfactorily with eight categories. An absolute minimum would be two categories – positive behaviour and negative behaviour – although observers may find some difficulties in allocating contributions given this limitation.

Figure 5.5 suggests a limited BA, using eight categories only, that will be found to be an acceptable compromise.

CATEGORIES	JOHN	MARY	FRED	TOTALS
PROPOSING				
SEEKING INFORMATION				
SUMMARIZING (particularly when observing a leader)				
DISAGREEING				
GIVING INFORMATION				
BLOCKING, DIFFICULTY STATING, ATTACKING				
INTERRUPTING				
OTHER BEHAVIOUR (add + when helpful, – when unhelpful)				
TOTALS				

Figure 5.5 *A limited BA form*

6

—

Other Methods of
Observing People

This chapter:

- considers other uses for Behaviour Analysis – one-to-one interactions
- discusses other methods of observing people – simple contribution scoring; directional sociograms
- identifies some general observation approaches – task process
  observation; specific activity observations; Fishbowl technique
- discusses observation strategies and aids.

OTHER USES FOR BEHAVIOUR ANALYSIS
IN PEOPLE OBSERVATION

Behaviour Analysis can be applied to one-to-one interactions as well
as group situations, and in fact is more flexible and easier to use in the
former. Usually the observer has to watch only two people, perhaps
three or four as a maximum, depending on the type of interaction – a
counselling interview would usually have two people, a negotiating
interaction might be more like the group situation. Also in one-to-one
interactions, because the BA task is less onerous for the observers they
are able to listen more carefully to what is being said. One criticism of
BA is that it only records the behaviour of the players, but there is
always a second aspect in an interaction – the progress to achievement
of the task. If observation of the process is required an analytical instrument designed for that purpose must be used, and, of course, as has
been mentioned earlier, the important aspect of non-verbal communication cannot be ignored. There is no single instrument capable of

recording all these aspects so, if observation and recording of all aspects is required, several observers, each looking at particular aspects, must be used.

As an example of one-to-one BA observation, let us use a job appraisal interview as the study case. The categories that an observer of practice appraisal interviews would want to consider would usually be more specific than for the general group described in the preceding chapter. Examples of relevant categories might be:

Prescribing	Suggesting
Building	Asking for ideas
Asking open questions	Asking closed questions
Asking multiple questions	Asking leading questions
Giving information	Supporting/agreeing
Disagreeing	Testing understanding
Summarizing	Shutting out
Other negative behaviour (blocking, attacking, difficulty stating)	

Although this list of categories is extensive because only two people are interacting, and in most cases only one person is speaking, the BA is not as difficult as it seems at first.

Figure 6.1 gives an example of a BA appraisal interview form with the contributions of the two participants entered, demonstrating the behaviour pattern of a not very effective interviewer. The interviewer obviously took a very prescriptive line and made little attempt to really involve the person being appraised. The interviewee made several attempts to break into the appraiser's monologues, but with little success, and slowly opted out of the interview.

Figure 6.2 gives an example of a more effective appraisal interview, with the interviewer taking very much the secondary role and allowing/encouraging the interviewee to speak and let their thoughts emerge.

OTHER METHODS OF ACTIVITY OBSERVATION

Behaviour Analysis is one of the most effective methods of behaviour observation, but it may be too costly in time and resources, both in the observation itself and in the essential subsequent feedback. There are other, simpler methods, but it must be noted that, precisely because of this simplicity, analysis will be less exact and complete. However, on occasions these and other more subjective instruments will suffice.

	APPRAISER	INTERVIEWEE
Prescribing	7	
Suggesting		1
Building		
Asking for ideas		1
Open questions	2	5
Closed questions	18	5
Multiple questions	9	
Leading questions	12	
Giving information	28	5
Supporting/agreeing	1	1
Disagreeing	14	14
Testing understanding		
Summarizing	1	
Negative behaviour	15	12
Shutting out	8	18
Totals	115	62

Figure 6.1 *An ineffective appraisal interview BA form*

	APPRAISER	INTERVIEWEE
Prescribing	1	
Suggesting		12
Building	8	
Asking for ideas	6	1
Open questions	12	8
Closed questions	2	3
Multiple questions		
Leading questions		
Giving information	8	25
Supporting/agreeing	9	8
Disagreeing		
Testing understanding	6	3
Summarizing	2	6
Negative behaviour	2	2
Shutting-out	1	2
Totals	57	70

Figure 6.2 *A more effective appraisal interview BA form*

Simple contribution scoring

This is the simplest instrument that can be used in behaviour activity observation. As its name implies, it scores the number of contributions made by the individuals in the group being observed. It does little more than this, although it can be extended somewhat to give further information. The recording form is simply a piece of paper on which the names of the participants are entered. As the interaction proceeds, as each person speaks a stroke is made against their name – five-bar gates can be used here as in full BA. At the end of the interaction the individual scores are totalled, and if you wish to express these as percentages, the individual scores are calculated against the group total. Figure 6.3 shows one of these scoring instruments that gives this information, the individual totals being the penultimate column, the individual percentages of the group total in the final column.

Name	Score		%
John	ℋℋ ℋℋ ℋℋ ℋℋ ℋℋ ℋℋ ℋℋ ℋℋ ℋℋ ℋℋ III	53	36
Fred	ℋℋ ℋℋ ℋℋ ℋℋ I	21	14
Charlie	ℋℋ III	8	6
Joan	III	3	2
Sam	ℋℋ ℋℋ ℋℋ	15	10
Mary	ℋℋ ℋℋ ℋℋ ℋℋ ℋℋ ℋℋ ℋℋ ℋℋ ℋℋ	45	31
Rita	I	1	1
Totals		146	100

Figure 6.3 *Simple contribution scoring*

The example in Figure 6.3 shows that we now know, rather than just suspect, that Rita spoke once only and Joan only three times. However, although these contributions may have been very important or significant the instrument cannot show this. Similarly with John and Mary: it is evident that they were high contributors, but many of these contributions may have been short or not relevant to the interaction. So, the instrument shows only basic details, but it may raise questions that must be answered – for example, if Rita's contribution was the most important one of the interaction, why did she/was she allowed to speak only once? Does the record suggest that John and Mary may have to be controlled more strictly to reduce the number of their contributions and allow others to have a more effective say?

Simple contribution scoring can be enhanced by showing the length of time each contribution lasted. Instead of putting a stroke down for each contribution, a stroke should be made for each 10 seconds of the contribution (10 seconds is quite easy to estimate with experience). A further variation can demonstrate the sequence of contributions in the interaction – instead of a stroke entry, the first person's contribution would be marked with 1; the next contribution 2; the next 3, etc.

Directional sociograms

Directional sociograms are an extension of simple contribution scoring and give information about the type of interaction and the flow pattern of the discussion.

The instrument consists initially of a blank sheet of paper on which circles are drawn showing the placing of the members of the interaction, with lines joining each member and a short line extending outwards from each one, as shown in Figure 6.4.

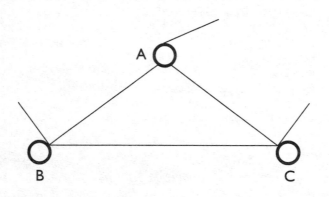

Figure 6.4   *Initial form of directional sociogram*

As the discussion proceeds, each time a member speaks an arrow is placed on the line to the person to whom the contribution is directed. If it is directed to the group as a whole, the arrow is placed on the 'external' line. Interruptions can be shown by bars across the line. Consequently the completed instrument shows:

- the number of contributions made by each individual
- the number of contributions made by the group
- the number of interruptions that occurred and who made them
- the flow of the interaction – who talked to whom.

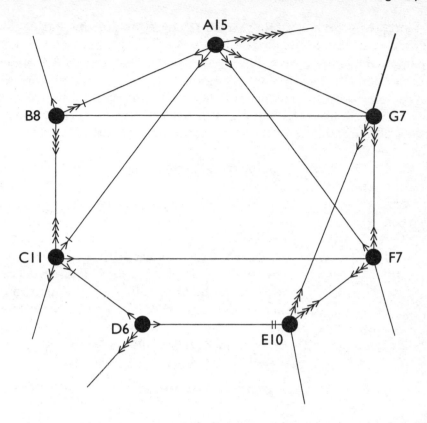

Figure 6.5 *Directional sociogram*

Figure 6.5 shows an example of a completed directional sociogram, the figures beside each circle being the number's total contributions, and the arrows showing the flow. A bar across the flow line indicates an interruption of the person at the other end of the line.

Figure 6.5 therefore shows that A (the group leader) spoke 15 times, 8 of which were to the group, and to each other member except D and E: not everybody responded. D was virtually isolated with nobody speaking directly to him and he was forced to make most of his contributions to the group (which ignored them!). E, F and G monopolized the discussion, forming a triad within the main group and speaking chiefly to each other. They made no contributions to the group as a whole and F spoke only once to the leader, A. B and C spoke mainly to each other, consequently forming another sub-group.

GENERAL OBSERVATION APPROACHES

There will be training and development occasions when a Behaviour Analysis type of instrument, whether as simple as the simple form or as complex as BA, is not appropriate or the trainer/observer does not want to use it. Instead, a more general observational approach can be used, although many of these can be combined with the analytical instruments.

Prior to an activity the trainer must decide which type of observation should be performed – verbal behaviours, non-verbal behaviours, task process, leadership and so on. This decision will point the way to the type of observation sheet that the observers will use. Verbal behaviours might be observed with BA if this complexity is wanted, or a modified BA with fewer, more general behaviour categories. A similar instrument (modified as necessary) might be chosen for non-verbal observation.

As the group – two people in a one-to-one situation or a full group of learners – takes part in the interaction, discussion and activity, they are observed by a selected observer or group of observers who write their comments on the relevant observations sheets.

Task process observation

Figure 6.6 gives an example of an observation sheet for observers looking at the specific processes in a negotiation. One observer group might look at one negotiation team, another at the other; if there are several observers looking at each team, one observer might look at one of the negotiators only, others at the other members.

Observation of behaviour in a specific type of activity

If behaviour is to be observed in a more general way than with BA when an interactive group are, for example, in a problem-solving/decision-making activity, the options include:

- observing the leader/chairperson alone
- observing the interaction between members alone
- observing both leader and members.

Many of the questions will be similar for both leader or member, the differences relating to the specific behaviours required of these roles. Figures 6.7 and 6.8 suggest checklists that can be used by the observers for both the leader and member roles.

OBSERVATION SHEET FOR TEAM A IN X NEGOTIATION

Process	High skill				Low skill	
Opening statement of negotiating event — aims, objectives	5	4	3	2	1	0
Comments:						
Offer of shopping list	5	4	3	2	1	0
Comments:						
Seeking others' shopping list	5	4	3	2	1	0
Comments:						
First objective raising	5	4	3	2	1	0
Comments:						
etc						

Figure 6.6 *Observation sheet for a negotiation activity*

CHECKLIST FOR OBSERVATION OF THE LEADER IN A PROBLEM-SOLVING ACTIVITY

Observe the group leader during the activity and make notes on her behaviours and how they relate to helping the effectiveness of the event. The following items suggest behaviours you should specifically look out for, but also comment on any other behaviours you feel are relevant.

How was the activity explained to the group?
Was there ample opportunity for clarification?
Unless pre-set, how were goals, aims and objectives set?
How did the leader set about organizing the activity?
To what extent were members given the opportunity to express their ideas?
To what extent did the leader take their views into account?
How were the final decisions made and by whom?
Were special expertise and resources determined within the group?
Was information about previous experience sought?
What style of leadership did the leader follow? Was this successful?
To what extent did the leader try to motivate the members?
How effective was the leader's communication with the group?
Did the leader utilize everybody in the event?
What were the good aspects of the leadership?
What were the less good aspects of the leadership?
On a scale of 6 (good) to 1 (poor) how would you rate the leader?

Any other comments about what the leader did or should have done:

Figure 6.7 *Leader's observation checklist*

CHECKLIST FOR OBSERVATION OF THE MEMBERS IN A
PROBLEM-SOLVING ACTIVITY

Observe the group members during the activity and make notes on their
behaviours and how they relate to helping or hindering the effectiveness of the
event. The following items suggest behaviours you should specifically look out
for, but also comment on any other behaviours you feel are relevant. Do not
try to make a note of everything, only behaviours that appear to be important
or significant.

Did the purpose of the event appear to be understood by the people involved?
Were any clarifying questions asked? Should they have been?
To what extent did the participants involve themselves in the organization for
    the activity?
To what extent did the members express their ideas?
How much did the leader take account of these suggestions?
To what extent did the members involve themselves in the final decisions?
Were the members' knowledge, skills, and expertise used effectively?
Was information about previous relevant experience volunteered?
How did the members react to the leader?
How motivated and enthusiastic were the members?
How effective was the group's communication with:

- the leader
- the other members?

Did everybody take an active part in the event?
What were the good aspects of the members' behaviours?
What were the less good aspects of the members' behaviours?
Was the task achieved? If so, how successfully?
On a scale of 6 (good) to 1 (poor), how would you rate the group in the
performance of this event?

Any other comments on events during the activity for which the members
were responsible?

Figure 6.8 *Members' observation checklist*

THE FISHBOWL

This is a very frequently used approach for the observation of both
task processes and human behaviours. The technique is used in a
training group event when a training task has to be performed: problem
solving, analytical discussion, ranking decision making etc.

Let us say that a training group of 12 learners has been given a controversial subject to discuss or a problem to solve. The first stage is to divide the group into two smaller ones of six each. One group of six is seated in a circle and perform the activity, coming to conclusions about the subject or providing solutions to the problem. The second group is seated round the outside of the group in a circle, in such a way that each member of group two has a clear view of one member of group one. As the activity proceeds the selected group one members are observed by their group two counterparts, their behaviour or part in the process being recorded, the observers using BA or a modified form, or a checklist related to the process involved.

At the end of the activity the group roles are reversed, the observers becoming the activity performers and the original performers becoming the observers using the same methods as with the initial 'fishbowl'. At the end of the second part of the activity the behaviours etc are reviewed and discussed.

OBSERVATION STRATEGIES AND AIDS

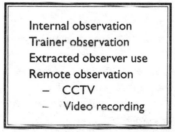

Internal observation
Trainer observation
Extracted observer use
Remote observation
    – CCTV
    – Video recording

Internal observation

There will be occasions when it is essential that some form of observation is used so that a review and feedback session can take place following the event, but where it is not relevant for the trainer to do this nor for people to be extracted from the group as observers. This can be performed by the participating members themselves, although it is the most suspect and unreliable form of observation. The dangers include the omission of learning points, misinterpretation of process events, failure to notice significant behaviours and, although these are serious, their omission is natural, particularly when the people are enthusiastically involved in what they are doing.

The maximum failure usually occurs at the end of the event if the group is simply asked to comment on what they saw. The result is usually either silence or very chaotic comments. If you intend to follow this path the members must be warned about their part in the observation: what they should be looking for, incidents that may occur for which they should be on the look-out etc.

A very effective method of preparing the members is to describe the observation at the start of the event and give them a checklist of processes and behaviours they could usefully look out for, and which they can use in the review at the end of the event. It is then essential to give them some time before the start of the event (the first session in a series of events) to identify as many items as possible on checklist that they need to look out for during the event. Two distinct reflection checklists can be identified – one for the leader of the event and one for the members. Figure 6.9 suggests a checklist for a leader's self-assessment and Figure 6.10 for the members.

---

1. What did you assess as the specific objectives for the event?
2. How successful do you feel you were in the achievement of these objectives?
3. What were the main problems you encountered and why did these occur?
4. How did you overcome the problems?
5. What did *you* do that hindered the process?
6. What behaviour or actions by the group members
   - hindered you and the performance of the task
   - helped you in the performance of the task?
7. If you had been a member, how differently would you have behaved or what would you have done?
8. If you had to repeat the activity, what changes would you make?
9. What have you learned from this experience?

Figure 6.9 *Leader's reflection checklist*

Trainer observation

In many ways this is, or should be the most effective observational approach, because the trainer is an expert in a wide range of training techniques, particularly in relation to the specific training being performed. Part of the professional training for trainers is in observation, review and feedback and they will, therefore, be in a more privileged position than untrained learners. This, of course, is the theory, as in practice the skills of trainers, and managers, varies widely.

1. Did the purpose of the event appear to be understood by a) you b) the other members?
2. Did you or the other members ask clarifying questions? If not, should they have been? How well were they answered?
3. To what extend did a) you b) the other members become involved in the organization for the activity? Would you have wanted more?
4. To what extent did you and the other members express their ideas?
5. How much did the leader take account of these suggestions?
6. To what extent were a) you b) the other members involved in the final decisions?
7. Were the members' knowledge, skills, and expertise used effectively?
8. Was information about previous relevant experience sought by the leader?
9. How did the members react to the leader?
10. How motivated and enthusiastic were the members?
11. How effective was the group's communication with the leader and the other members? How well did you communicate?
12. Did everybody take an active part in the event? How active were you?
13. What were the good aspects of the members' behaviours? Can you identify any of your own?
14. What were the less good aspects of the members' behaviours? Can you identify any of your own?
15. Was the task achieved? If so, how successfully?
16. On a scale of 6 (good) to 1 (poor), how would you rate the group in the performance of this event? How would you rate yourself?

Figure 6.10 *Member's reflection checklist*

The observation by the trainer should be realistic, relevant, unbiased and comprehensive, and, depending on the skill of the trainer, accurate in all respects.

Skill to this level is asking a lot of a trainer, who is after all just a person and consequently has value judgements, likes, dislikes, biases and blind spots, and may consciously or unconsciously allow these to influence any observations. If these are obvious, the review and feedback may be rejected by the learners, however accurate they might be. These and other dangers of trainer observation can be:

> General people failings
> 'If you were me'
> Over- or under-criticism
> Multi-group observation
> Unsolicited intervention

General people failings. Even the most experienced observer cannot be 100 per cent effective. Private value judgements can intrude in what should be a neutral observation and comment. Events can be incompletely seen and consequently the causes and effects misinterpreted. A trainer might have a blind spot for certain actions, always omitting these from the observation and feedback, although they may have been obvious events.

'If you were me'. Because you as the trainer or manager are more of an expert than the learners there is always the danger that comments should be prefaced by this dangerous statement. This is dangerous because you are not the learners, and you are not doing what they are doing. You could so easily believe that you would have performed differently (ie, better!) and this would emerge in the review.

Over- or under-criticism. It is often difficult for the observer to decide how 'hard' or 'soft' to be with the learners, particularly without any knowledge of how they will react to your eventual review. Too hard and they will complain that you have been too critical; too soft and they could accuse you of not observing with sufficient awareness and acuity, or that you are being patronizing and trying to protect them.

Multi-group observation. If you are the only facilitator you can only be in one place at a time. If the learning group has been divided into a number of smaller groups you will be torn between staying with one group (the other groups may complain about this as you will have no way of helping them via your observations), and moving from one group to another with the danger of missing some significant events. This could give rise in the eventual review to a group's response that, 'Oh, we did that when you weren't with us.'

One solution would be to have several trainers, but this is not always possible, so you may have to decide to withdraw some learners to act as observers – see the dangers of this later!

Unsolicited intervention. You have to make an initial decision about your role as observer and interventionist. As an observer you will be frequently tempted, when things are going wrong, to intervene and put the interactors on the correct track. It may, of course, be necessary on occasions for you to do this.

- They are going so badly off course that the interaction will be such a failure as to cause damage.
- There is insufficient event time to let them 'sort themselves out'.

But on most occasions it is not your role to intervene, and more learning will result from the participants working out their own solutions.

If, however, you have to intervene:

- do not tell them that they are going wrong
- do not tell them what they should do.

A more effective approach would be to suggest that they:

- might consider whether they are following an effective path
- might like to consider such-and-such as an alternative approach.

Extracted observer use

In many cases of observation the most effective approach will be to extract some of the participants from the learning group and use them as observers. This approach will relieve the lone trainer from the problems of multi-group observation and such observers can be most effective, particularly if they receive some training. Without this training, or at least guidance and advice, too much may be missed and the review and/or feedback becomes ineffective. However, even without fully accurate and comprehensive observation, the remainder of the group may more easily accept criticism from their peers than from the trainer. Otherwise, they may fall foul of the dangers inherent in the trainer-observer role.

Training will obviously eat into the event time, but it need not necessarily be over extensive, except perhaps in the case of BA training. The significant criterion for effective learner-observer training is:

A thorough briefing before the interaction to observed. This will include information about the interaction itself, their roles and responsibilities, and comprehensive guidance on what they should be looking for – checklists and questionnaires can be used to ease this part of the task. The learners can be:

- given a separate session on observation skills and requirements before the start of any interactive events that will need to be observed
- formed into a group of observers for a particular interaction and briefed while, perhaps, the participants are reviewing their roles in the event
- given time to read the briefs for the interaction and examine their checklists and questionnaires, possibly making their own decisions about various aspects.

It will naturally be too much to expect that the group of relatively untrained observers will perform as good a job as an experienced trainer-observer, but these failings must be accepted by both the trainer and the learning group in the absence of any alternatives. Errors and omissions can, in fact, form the basis of a sound, reflective, controlled discussion after the event when the feedback is being given. I include 'controlled' because this discussion could so easily degenerate into a fight if substantial disagreements emerged.

Remote observation – CCTV and video recording

Live observation by observers in the same room as the interactors (frequently very close to them) can be off-putting for the participants, and this is commonly used as an excuse when performance has not been as good as it should have been – 'It seemed unnatural with X sitting near us.' The answer is to move the observers to where they can see but not be seen. Some years ago, this was achieved by using one-way glass. The observers sat on the 'see-through' side of the glass and could observe everything that was going on, unseen by the participants, and hearing the verbal interaction by means of an audio link. This had serious disadvantages because, although the interactors could not see the observers, they knew they were behind the glass, and the window itself was a distracting and upsetting factor. On past training events in which I have been involved rarely did participants ever come to terms with the 'fly on the wall'– shades of 'big brother is watching you' and the one-way windows in immigration offices at airports.

Closed-circuit television (CCTV) technology has replaced the window, but unfortunately it has not completely dispelled all the original fears and, in fact, has added some. The set-up for the use of CCTV is a room for the interactors to take part in a role play, discussion or other activity, with no other person present in the room. Mounted on a wall, usually high up in one corner, is a television camera that transmits via a cable link the audio-visual pickup from the room to an observing room. This latter could be a considerable distance away from the interaction room. The observer(s) watch the action live on a monitor in the observation room and, at the same time, the activity is being recorded on a video recorder. This is an excellent medium for use in the review and feedback session, as a stand-alone feedback instrument or as a support/supplement to the human observers.

One very significant factor in the use of CCTV and video recording of the interactions is that a permanent, accurate record of what actually happened is produced, and this can be used very effectively in a variety of review and feedback sessions.

Three principal problems are found when using CCTV:

1. The awareness of the participants of the camera watching and recording their movements and speech can be unnerving, and many learners comment that its presence made the whole situation feel unnatural and that they were unable to perform naturally.
2. The movement of the camera as it focuses or changes direction to watch particular interactors indifferent parts of the room can be intrusive and unsettling.
3. Reversing the first problem, some people will over-respond to the camera and, instead of behaving naturally in the situation, will 'play to the camera'.

Unfortunately there is little that can be done about the first problem, linked with the second – the camera is there, and although modern cameras are very small they can still be seen once the participants know they are there. In custom-built suites it may be possible to position the camera in such a way that it is less obtrusive but can still swivel. Even then, the participants still know it is there and watching them. One quite successful approach is to locate the camera behind a plastic dome that enables the camera to 'see' but not be seen. The participants know the camera is behind the dome, but it is at its lowest level of visibility and obtrusiveness.

The second problem links with camera-shyness, and probably the most effective way of dealing with both of these is to ignore them as far as possible. It has always amazed me how quickly participants will become used to and forget about the camera, even though they were very aware initially. Once they have relaxed natural actions soon start. This familiarity can be aided by always having a camera visible, even if it is not being used. In general rooms a camera on a tripod can serve this purpose, as well as being used practically to record group discussions, presentations, activities and so on.

TRIADS

One very common and useful approach in the observation of one-to-one people interactions is the triad approach, a technique that emphasizes the value of an external observer when people are immersed in interactions.

The usual time to use this approach is when two people have a face-to-face interaction, such as a practice counselling interview. Present, close, and *almost* taking part in the interaction is a third person, the observer. In the triad's simplest form the third person is a normal observer who, at the end of the interaction, reviews it with the participants and gives feedback on their behaviour and processes as seen from the external, neutral viewpoint. But the triad approach can be taken further than this, the observer taking a more active role. In the one-to-one interaction the first person speaks, but before the second person responds they have to summarize what has been said, then make their response. The triadic observer can intervene if the summary is incorrect or incomplete and these points are not taken up by the original speaker. The second speaker then makes a contribution that is first summarized by the first before responding to the contribution, with the triadic observer continuing to be the referee.

Some learners, and indeed trainers, feel that the interventionist approach of the triad makes the interaction unnatural and disjointed, although there can be no doubt that the particular process ensures full understanding and reaction.

One final point on observation: if you are going to utilize the resources of a facilitator and/or the participants, with or without audio-visual assistance, the process is wasted if it is not used. The place for the use of observational comments is in a review and feedback session following the interaction. This type of session will be discussed in later chapters when specific interactions are being considered, as some interactive events require different forms of review.

SECTION TWO

Specific Aspects of People Skills

7

—

Coaching skills – I

This chapter:

- describes coaching as a significant aspect of developing people and people skills
- offers the first two stages of a structure to help coaches.

Coaching is possibly the most significant and important approach to people skills, certainly more so than the remoteness of training courses or even open learning programmes completed at work. It takes place in the work environment, controlled by someone the learner knows well, and utilizes work situations, problems and projects. It is the most personal of any form of people skills, but tends to be underutilized, frequently due to the lack of knowledge of and/or skill in coaching of the manager or other coach. The potential coach can readily overcome these deficiencies through effective training.

WHAT IS COACHING?

Coaching can be defined as:

- The development of the ability, skills and experience of people by giving them the opportunity of training and development at work, utilizing systematically planned and stretching tasks of real work as the learning vehicles. These activities are coupled with continuous appraisal and counselling by the responsible coach.
- The practical advantage of coaching is that it avoids learners having to leave their work to attend training events, instead using work situations for the learning process.

The word 'development' is used because coaching can range from people who have few or no skills to more experienced people who require the topping-up of existing skills, and the development of an individual beyond their present job requirements.

'Ability' and 'skills' are those job competences that the learner must possess to perform their job effectively, or to prepare them for other, higher levels of work.

The definition stresses than coaching is systematic rather than haphazard, because the learning takes place at work as opposed to the disciplined, remote, non-work environment of the training course, and must be strictly controlled to ensure that it fits in with and does not disturb the essential work flow.

'Tasks of real work' form the basis of coaching, as the training tasks the learner has to perform are not artificial, training course tasks, but the real work of the department.

'Planning' involves the construction of a systematic programme of early, easier tasks for the unskilled learner, progressing to increasingly difficult and complex tasks, the starting point being assessed by the existing skill of the learner.

'Appraisal' and 'counselling' are essential parts of the process, at different stages, the coach taking an active part in helping the learner and assessing the achievements from both the learning and the work completion aspects. These contacts will help the coaches in their management roles in people skills in other areas of assessment and appraisal and will accustom the learners to direct learning contacts and contacts with their bosses.

WHAT AND WHO IS A COACH?

Most people think of a coach in the sporting context, an analogy not too distant from the coach at a work establishment. In sport, the coach usually has a dual role: to provide guidance and advice and devise practical ways in which individuals can improve their skills and performance; and to weld a number of individuals with various and varying skills into an effective working team. This parallels the description of the coach at work, although in the sporting world the coach is identified as having this specific role.

In industry and commerce, many managers and supervisors have held, and many still do, that anything connected with training and development is the direct responsibility of the training department, not the line manager. Sometimes this is their real belief, but it can also stem from their lack of confidence in their abilities to introduce and practise coaching. There will always, of course, be occasions when coaching is not possible because of time and resource constraints, but too often these are used as an excuse, not a reason, for not coaching.

Who coaches?

- The manager, as described earlier, *must* be the person *responsible* for coaching. However, this does not necessarily mean that it must be the manager only who *does* the coaching.
- Managers are in the ideal position to focus their power on the development of their staff because:
  - this is an inescapable responsibility
  - they are *responsible* for the type of work that can be used in the coaching
  - there should be a relationship between manager and staff that encourages this approach – or provides the opportunity for it to be developed.
- The manager cannot do it all, and full use of local experts (including junior staff with the expertise) should be made, under management overall control.

Although the coaching role should fall squarely on the shoulders of the manager, the training department can give support, for example when certain aspects of training or expertise are not readily available at the workplace.

COACHING REQUIREMENTS

- The manager does not have to be a 'star' in the activity for which coaching is being applied, rather their strength lies in their ability to direct the development, build and maintain the learner's motivation to perform, and provide the practical opportunities for learning and development.
- The coach must be willing to follow the coaching through to its conclusion, whatever pressures may arise.
- The coach must be able to recognize and analyse learning situations, select them for the specific learner(s) and appraise the performance at the end of the assignment.
- If coaching skills are not already possessed, every effort and opportunity must be made to attain them quickly in order that the coaching of others can proceed.
- The coach must be willing to delegate many aspects of the coaching to 'experts' and training specialists.

- The coach or manager must also be prepared to delegate work and the authority to go with it, but retain final responsibility for its effective completion.

Managers should always remember that coaching is a permanent and ongoing process, particularly when there is a change of staff in their departments, and because in most organizations work demands are far from static.

WHY COACHING?

Initiating and maintaining coaching may raise the question of whether coaching is the most effective medium for the training and development of people. If coaching is not the chosen medium, the traditional means of providing 'learning' opportunities for staff include the following.

- Send them on a training course. These can offer good learning opportunities, with experts and specialists available to support the learner, but problems may arise in the 'artificiality' of the course and eventual transfer of the learning back at work.
- Sit them with 'Nellie/Fred' and expect them to pick up the work sufficiently speedily and efficiently to enable them to start productive work. This will only work if 'Nellie' is also an effective trainer or is given training for this role, practises appropriate on-the-job training methods and if sufficient time and resources are made available.
- Provide an open or distance learning package. These can present difficulties for the learner learning alone – remoteness or absence of support, impossibility of immediate discussions for clarification and problem solving, and/or time not available or not given at work. Some of these problems can be solved to some extent by personal or telephone contact with a supporting expert, or, as is available with an increasing number of packages, via e-mail or the Internet.

THE BENEFITS OF COACHING

Organizations and coaches need to be convinced of the value of coaching, and the benefits include:

Improved individual performance
Improved team performance
Cumulative improved performance for the organization
People better informed and aware
People better equipped for change
Innovation encouraged
Increased job satisfaction
More managerial time available to manager
More systematic managerial succession
Learning performed at workplace
Learners do not have to leave work/home
Uses real work, hence credibility and easy translation
    of learning
Coaches themselves develop skills

These benefits can be allocated to specific areas.

To the organization

Organizations have a greater chance of success when their workforce is efficient and effective, constructively managed and supervised and given the opportunity to develop. None of this just happens – people need to be trained to perform their tasks and also to look to development. Standing still, either as an organization or an individual, leads to regression and lack of achievement. Specific benefits include:

- improved staff performance without the high costs of time away from the job and courses
- the workforce becomes more flexible and skilled and potential is developed internally
- improved working relationships with better communications and interactions
- a greater openness in the organization
- change processes become easier
- costs of coaching are less than training, internal or external

Benefits to the learner

- increased skill, confidence, flexibility and self-reliance
- use of real tasks gives a feeling of greater involvement, commitment and job satisfaction
- opportunities are given to grow at work, to become more experienced and to obtain an insight into work at higher levels

- people develop into active learners who look for more developmental opportunities

Benefits to the coach

- a wider opportunity to use the skills of people more effectively, saving time and money and improving a team environment
- more effective control over and greater flexibility in change situations
- with a fully developed staff, work and relationships run more smoothly
- development or reinforcement of personal skills.

WHAT DOES COACHING ACHIEVE?

According to Megginson and Boydell (1979), coaching achieves movement in four major areas:

1. *Dependence to independence*. Increased skill as a result of coaching gives the learner more confidence and consequently they can perform more effectively as an individual.
2. *Superficial knowledge and application to in-depth knowledge and skilled application*. This means quite simply that they become more skilled and mature at work, which helps them to see the job as more interesting and challenging.
3. *Ignorance to understanding*. Coaching is more about development than training and will not only increase the learners' skills but also their understanding of their place in the organization.
4. *Predictability and constraint to an acceptance of ambiguity and risk*. If your staff are held back, their results will be constrained. When you coach them you will:
   - increase their skill and confidence
   - encourage their increased willingness to be creative
   - encourage them to develop systems and procedures beyond the existing ones
   - encourage them in general to take risks, and make them able to assess when these risks can be taken.

THE STRUCTURE OF COACHING

A coaching process will benefit from a structured approach. In the following structure, seven stages are identified:

Stage one	Recognizing the need
Stage two	Identifying the opportunity
Stage three	Setting the coaching climate
Stage four	Meeting the learner
Stage five	Agreeing the assignment reviews and final review
Stage six	Implementation
Stage seven	Review

STAGE ONE: RECOGNIZING THE NEED

Whom to coach

Although desirable, it is not feasible to coach *all* your staff *all* the time. In theory, everybody is a potential candidate and each should be considered when coaching is being planned. In addition to possible time constraints, however, not everybody wants to progress or develop, thus narrowing the field, but be careful about making assumptions about people's needs.

People for coaching consideration will include:

> ■ People who are not performing to the required standards
> ■ People who have to perform a new job or range of jobs in their employment, either because of job rotation or the introduction of new work.
> ■ People who have shown potential for development and promotion
> ■ Frustrated people

The common reaction to the question 'whom to coach?' is to concentrate on poor performers, the easiest group to identify and one for which successful coaching will bring the best, immediate benefits. For this group, coaching is the specific alternative to training courses and the majority of people will welcome (a) the opportunity for development and (b) not being required to go away for training.

But coaching has a much wider application than remedial training and development. Few sections of work remain stable and new tasks and procedures are frequently introduced. More often than not these have to be implemented quickly but have not usually been planned with training in mind. Coaching is the ideal mechanism in these cases as the learning must move hand in hand with the work implementation, and there is no guarantee that a relevant training course exists or is immediately available. The added advantage is that transfer of knowledge is much easier when the learning uses the actual work in the process. This might seem to be an opportunity to develop inexperienced or poorer performers, but usually the urgency of the work implementation means that the more experienced people will be trained first. But when the initial pressure has eased the coach must start to introduce other workers to the new tasks as part of their developmental training.

Effective and caring management and organizations should always be looking for opportunities to improve and develop their people. Succession is a process that should always be borne in mind – staff will be looking towards promotion and/or job movement and coaching can be valuable in preparing them for this. High flyers are prime candidates for grooming for promotion through coaching and should be encouraged in every way – after all, one day one of them may be *your* boss.

The final group contains workers who are effective and satisfactory, but possibly frustrated, often because their current job has ceased to challenge them or perhaps through lack of promotion. Additional training through coaching to include fitting them for more demanding work will often help to reduce the frustration and at the same time widen the individual's skills.

Successful coaching can benefit the manager as much as the individual. The wider the range of tasks the worker can perform, and more effectively, the less the pressure on the boss and the higher the success level of the work unit. This success will reflect on the boss, who will be recognized as an effective manager and coach, whose own progress and development is then assisted. This should obviously not be the prime reason for coaching, but it is a legitimate side-effect.

Establishing the coaching need

Before any individual or group can commence development programmes through coaching it is necessary to identify the skills, knowledge and attitudes they need to acquire, the standards required for these skills, and the timescale required and available. The basic procedure is:

ESTABLISH THE TRAINING AND COACHING NEEDS –
those of the individual, the work unit and the organization
SET THE COACHING OBJECTIVES

Establishing the training/coaching needs is a subject that requires much more space than is available here, so the process will be dealt with in summary only. There are three basic stages in assessing an individual's training needs:

1. Achieving a complete analysis of the job being performed or to be performed by means of the production of a *job specification* or *job/ task analysis*. This will determine the types and ranges of the skills, knowledge and attitudes needed to perform the job satisfactorily.
2. Identification of the existing skill etc of the individual, resulting in a *person specification.*
3. Describing the difference between what the individual can do and what the job requires. This gap is the *training need*, training and coaching following to bridge the gap.

A number of techniques exist by which these aspects are identified and analysed – task analysis, observation, interview, questionnaire etc. Several useful books have been published that describe in detail these approaches (eg, Rae, 1997, Gower) and the coach or other training need researcher is referred to these publications.

A training matrix

Once the training needs of the organization, work unit and individuals have been identified and analysed, the manager/coach will find that a matrix of the training needs of all his or her staff forms a useful checklist. A simple matrix is shown in Figure 7.1. This can be used in a variety of ways, one of which is to head the vertical columns with the skills to be recorded. The horizontal rows are used for the individuals in the group. Existing skills are plotted for each individual, and a code can be used for ease of identification. For example, * signifies 'can do', and X 'can't do yet'. The skill level can be further defined with:

* = has knowledge of the skill, but is not yet a practitioner
** = can perform the skill, but only with difficulty or in a limited way
*** = can perform the skill well.

NAME	SKILLS							
	A	B	C	D	E	F	G	H
1	*	*	*	*	X	X	*	*
2	***	**	**	***	X	X	***	**
3								
4								
5								
6								

Figure 7.1 *A training skills matrix*

The training needs will stand out clearly in such a matrix, particularly if the Xs are entered in a different colour to the *s, and will help the coach determine the coaching priorities.

Setting coaching objectives

If the job or task analysis has been performed effectively it can be used to specify the coaching objectives, ie statements of what individuals will be able to do as a result of the coaching. These give the learner a clear picture of what is expected of them at the end of the coaching process, and enable the coach to determine the most effective methods to be used and recognize when the required learning has been achieved. Objectives must be written down to avoid misunderstandings and copies held by both the learner and the coach.

Coaching objectives should be clear and easily understood and this can be achieved by following three simple guidelines:

> 1. What the learner will be able to do
> 2. The standards of achievement
> 3. The conditions for achievement

The guideline describes in clear and comprehensive terms what the learner will be able to do at the end of the coaching, in terms of behaviour, performance and task achievement.

The standards of achievement should be defined accurately, in objective and measurable terms wherever possible. Objectivity and measurement are not always feasible, particularly in the more people oriented application of skills, but guidance maximum should be given, even within these constraints. Objective tasks can be measured objectively; subjective tasks can be assessed subjectively.

A simple example of a coaching objective using these guidelines is:

At the end of the coaching assignment, the learner 'X' will be able to type technical reports, letters and invoices, at a speed of 80 words per minute, with an initial accuracy of 98 per cent, using the Widget electronic typewriter.

STAGE TWO: IDENTIFYING THE OPPORTUNITY

Selecting coaching projects

A principal advantage of coaching is that most of the opportunities will be found in the day-to-day operation of the job. These can be summarized as:

```
 1.  Day-to-day work of the section
 2.  Following mistakes, failures or setbacks
 3.  Following successes and achievements
 4.  Planned delegation
 5.  Relief cover
 6.  Promotion or career development
 7.  Secondments or departmental moves
 8.  Projects, assignments, research, etc
 9.  Following training
10.  Meeting attendance
11.  Introduction of new work
```

1. *Day-to-day work of the section.* As a manager you will come into contact with the people you manage every day in the course of normal duties. Every contact is an opportunity for coaching, whether it is asking for a job to be done, seeking or discussing progress reports, or dealing with errors or omissions. Even the smallest task, if it is developing the person, is worth considering in the context of coaching.
2. *Following mistakes, failures or setbacks.* These should wherever possible be turned into positive, learning opportunities. This not only helps the person responsible to understand what has gone wrong and how to avoid it in the future, but a coaching approach can help to restore the individual's confidence. The aim should be to take this

action immediately, a major benefit as opposed to the worker waiting to take the problem to a training course.

3. *Following successes and achievements.* Coaching is not only about using negative work events, although significant learning from recognizing and analysing our mistakes can be achieved. We should be able to benefit also from our successes – what happened, who did what, how was it done, why did this approach succeeded etc – and a coaching approach will help people to take the opportunity to learn from these discussions. In addition, if people are aware that the boss recognizes and will comment on success as well as failure, self-confidence and motivation could increase and improve the boss-worker relationship.

4. *Planned delegation.* In delegation, some of the boss's work is passed on to another person to perform. Delegation is an integral part of coaching and can be used as an important learning event rather than simply as a work distribution exercise.

5. *Relief cover.* Work has to continue in the absence of a manager or supervisor and coaching can mean that there is always somebody available to ensure that this happens. The 'deputy' has to have the ability to undertake certain of the manager's tasks as well as decide what should be performed and what should be held back. Such decisions require a number of skills and abilities additional to the person's normal range and this coaching approach will need considerable care and attention.

6. *Promotion or career development.* Any change of job, promotion or imminent promotion can be ideal opportunities for coaching. Most new work, whether at a higher level as a result of promotion or as encouragement for career development, or simply new work in job rotation, is very suitable for coaching use.

7. *Secondments or departmental moves.* Some of your staff may sometimes be seconded to another area of work, either to help out in a crisis or as part of a career development plan. Similarly staff from other areas may be transferred temporarily to your work unit. Both of these are opportunities for coaching. A mutual coaching plan might be agreed with the manager of the importing or exporting work unit, and the coaching continued on the return of the worker to their base by application of their new skills etc in their 'home' environment.

8. *Projects, assignments, research etc.* These may be ongoing or one-off events and can be significant learning opportunities, particularly if they form part of a planned series of coaching assignments. They can offer the opportunity of giving the learner almost complete

control over all aspects of the project, bearing in mind that the manager still has the ultimate responsibility for the task.

9. *Following training*. On the return of a member of staff from training, coaching can be used in two ways. First, the returned learner can develop others by passing on what they have learned, for example in a presentation or teach-in. Second, in order to support and extend the training, opportunities must be made available for the learner to practise the techniques learned on the training course.

10. *Meeting attendance*. Sometimes there will be meetings that you should attend but are unable to. A representative can attend in your place, as suggested for relief cover, not simply to report back on the meeting but also to act for you, having been coached in the extent of their authority. Or individuals can attend meetings in your place even if you are available, to give them this type of experience, and perhaps a wider understanding of your role, that of the department and the organization.

11. *Introduction of new work*. Apart from the opportunities for coaching assignments once new work is introduced, people can be assigned to roles in the introduction itself and in this way individuals are helped to feel ownership of the work from the start and develop a pride and resolution to succeed.

Coaching for specific groups of people

The selection of a coaching project will depend on both the reasons for coaching and the needs of the individuals concerned. Decisions to coach can be made at any time – at a job appraisal review; during day-to-day observation; with particular identification of a need in an individual, perhaps demonstrated by lack of interest or boredom; following comments by the individual of a specific need etc. The first step is a mutual identification of the need and agreement of the way in which it can be satisfied. Some specific types of individual require coaching and each needs a different form. These types include:

> The poor performer
> The developer
> The high flyer

The poor performer

Here, the obvious choices for coaching will be areas of work that are not being performed effectively and in which the workers are not sufficiently skilled. A coaching approach will use the jobs themselves as the training medium, helping the learners to realize that the training is directly related to their performance and progress at work. This will ensure that the training is taken seriously as a learning approach and refers to the 'real world' rather than being attempted on a training course, which can often be seen as remote from actual work.

With these learners the *level* of the coaching assignment can often be a problem. If the level is seen by the learner as too low the approach may be rejected, as it may be felt that the coaching is simply a ruse to get them to work. Too high and the learner might fail, with a resultant loss of confidence and motivation to continue to improve and progress.

The most common failing in coaching, particularly in remedial coaching (although the same remarks apply to developmental coaching), is to give the learner too large a chunk of work or learning to perform. Remember the 'elephant diet' – don't try to eat it in one piece, cut it up into smaller, digestible portions'. Break the tasks down into identifiable, realistic, manageable steps with which the learner will be able to cope without too much difficulty, but not with too much ease. An example might be a statistics project – this could be broken down into monitoring records, collecting information, collating the figures, completing the statistical return, creating illustrative graphics, analysing the results, making recommendations etc.

The developer

The developmental coaching approach demands a more discriminating identification of tasks that are going to be the most helpful, rather than the obvious tasks of remedial coaching. The individual is assumed to be performing effectively, but this may not continue because they are not being stretched or challenged and are starting to look for more demanding work. This suggests that the coaching projects should be somewhat different from the learner's normal tasks. They might be other tasks in the work unit which the person has not had the opportunity to perform, or ones performed by people who are at the next stage in the organizational ladder. The former tasks must be progressive, realistic and in areas to which the learner might move. Care must be taken with the latter to avoid any feeling by the job holder that they are being eased out of their job.

A learner's colleagues can be useful in this approach: if the individual knows little about computer work and there is a colleague who is a computer specialist, the latter can pass on their skills. Incidentally, there is a second coaching opportunity here – the 'expert' is given the opportunity to develop training skills (it may be necessary to give them some coaching or training in this before the original coaching project is started). The more that others, particularly colleagues, can be used in these ways the less the direct demand on the manager who then has time to consider other coaching needs.

The high flyer

These people may be looking for your job! This is one of the reasons why coaching is not performed as frequently as it should be – the coach may feel that the more skills the staff are given the nearer their skills level to his or her own. Provided that you do not fear younger, up-and-coming people, you should welcome this motivation to develop them, to your level or beyond. Tasks and projects for this group of people suggest themselves readily. They can be given tasks, complete with authority under your final responsibility, that you might normally do yourself. For example, if you have to complete a complex and extensive report the learners can be given sections to do, perhaps relating to work with which they have had little or no experience. They would have to gather the information, collate and analyse it to the stage where it could be included in the main report. This not only gives them experience in other work but enables them to assess the type of work you do, the pressures on you and the level of your responsibility.

The selection of suitable coaching approaches and projects is not simple, and demands of the coach considerable knowledge of the individuals, the jobs available and the range of coaching techniques. One of the principal keys to successful coaching is discussion and agreement with the learner about the way progress can be achieved. Even the poor performers can make a significant contribution to these discussions, as one of the reasons why they perform below par might be the lack of opportunity or encouragement given to them to make suggestions.

The next chapter deals with the remaining five stages of the coaching structure.

8

Coaching Skills – 2

This chapter:

■ continues the description of the stages of the structure of coaching, namely stages three to seven.

A seven-stage structure for effective coaching was introduced in Chapter 7 and stages one and two described. The remaining stages are:

Stage three   Setting the coaching climate
Stage four   Meeting the learner
Stage five   Agreements for assignment reviews and the final review
Stage six   Implementation
Stage seven   The final review

By now we know whom we are going to coach, what our objectives are for the approach and which tasks will be used.

STAGE THREE: SETTING THE COACHING CLIMATE

Coaching, like any effective technique, needs extensive planning and preparation in order to be successful. Setting the climate is part of this preparation and this is something that must be developed, perhaps over a considerable period, to include mutual trust, support and understanding between learners and coach and between peers.

The coach must be prepared to demonstrate an open and honest interest in, a sincere intention of involvement with, and a helpful approach to people development. Without this interaction between the learner and coach the process may fail and the position could be worse than if it had never started. Honesty is essential, as a devious or insincere coach will soon be suspected or recognized.

The coach does not have to take on a 'holier than thou' attitude but, if they expect people to try to improve and develop they must set high standards of work and behaviour themselves.

A good coaching climate requires:

> Setting high performance standards
> Agreeing quantified standards
> Regular review of standards
> Creating personal development expectations
> Regularly reviewing job descriptions and practice
> Confirming that it is ok to seek help
> Encouraging creative risk taking
> Encouraging learning from mistakes
> Making coaching an ongoing process
> Developing an atmosphere of openness and trust

Setting high performance standards. Coaches and managers cannot motivate the potential learners – they can only do this themselves as motivation comes from within – but they can create a climate in which motivation can develop (see Maslow's and Herzberg's models described in Chapter 5).

Agreeing quantified standards and regular review of standards. The coach and the learners must be fully aware of and conversant with the standards required of jobs, task, levels and roles, and there must be a regular and constant review to ensure (a) that everybody is aware of the relevant standards and (b) that the standards are up to date with organizational requirements. The likelihood of staff working towards these standards will be greater if they have been set by interactive agreement rather than imposition.

Creating personal development expectations. People will not grow or want to grow if they do not believe that there are benefits in their doing so. Regular meetings on a one-to-one basis to discuss informally their progression and development will help to create a good atmosphere, but expectations must only be raised if there is going to be an opportunity for achieving them. The mini- or interim appraisal can be a useful occasion for discussing these expectations.

Regularly reviewing job descriptions and practice. Work practices, scope, procedures and attitudes change, and a regular review of the accurateness of current situations should be made, not left until the annual appraisal. A useful arrangement can be to give the post-holders responsibility for maintaining and updating references to the areas for which they are responsible, and perhaps convening meetings with other job-holders to compare roles and standards – a useful coaching tactic.

Confirming that it is OK to seek help. A new coaching atmosphere can take some time to develop and in many cases the existing staff attitude will be one of 'I'd better not ask for help on this as I will be disclosing that I am not fully up to my job'. This attitude can only be changed by the manager/coach's actual and repeated demonstration that asking for help will be looked on favourably, but not asking when necessary, with subsequent failure, will be viewed rather differently.

Encouraging creative risk taking. People's views on taking risks are generally the same as in asking for help, the traditional attitude being 'Play safe. Don't take too many risks as I could be blamed for failure and suffer as a result'. Again the manager/coach should openly encourage considered risk taking, at the same time showing that, if the risk fails, it will be looked on as a learning experience and not an occasion for discipline.

Encouraging learning from mistakes. When mistakes are made, the coach should discuss the occasion with the person(s) concerned, perhaps asking:

What went wrong?
How did it go wrong?
What were the consequences?
Could the error have been avoided? How?
What would you do if a similar situation arose?

A discussion of this nature, without heavy-handed discipline, will openly demonstrate the value of reflecting on errors and turning them into a learning situation.

There will of course be occasions when this highly supportive approach will not be appropriate, for example when uncalculated risks have been taken – and failed, when errors of a repetitive nature are still made (particularly following a coaching discussion), and so on; but if the opportunity presents itself as one for coaching rather than discipline, it should be taken.

Making coaching an ongoing process. The manager cannot initiate a coaching climate only to suspend it, restart it and suspend it again, or simply initiate it for one period of time. It must be ongoing, part of the overall atmosphere of the work unit. At the annual appraisal interview, this ongoing attitude can be expressed and demonstrated with the person concerned, and mini- or interim appraisals can help to develop the same atmosphere. The coaching climate can be developed in staff, group or team meetings, which will be epitomized by their openness and frankness – on the part of both the manager and staff. Meetings that are concerned with people and their needs, rather than just business meetings, can be held, and an ideal coaching climate will be seen to have been achieved if people openly disclose that they are having difficulties, and supportive suggestions are made by others about how these can be resolved.

Developing an atmosphere of openness and trust. This is probably the most difficult to achieve, but the most essential part of the coaching climate. Without this, little real advance will be made. Openness and trust are emotive aspects for both the manager and the staff, and involve considerable risks on both sides. Success will not be immediate, and may never be 100 per cent, although this should always be the aim. The manager/coach must practise these attitudes to the maximum extent possible, at all times, demonstrating them practically so that they will be seen to be sincere and will be accepted. Remember the saying that you can please some of the people some of the time, but not all the people all of the time.

STAGE FOUR: MEETING THE LEARNER

The planning meeting with the learner who is to be involved in the coaching project is one of the most important parts of the whole coaching process. This initial meeting will benefit significantly from a planned and structured approach, allowing for flexibility according to the person and the circumstances.

This first meeting should not come as a surprise to the learner with whom, apart from a group discussion in the unit, other contact will have been made – informal discussions, appraisal interviews etc. To prepare the learner for the meeting the coach should suggest, some days beforehand, that the learner might wish to think about the process so that progress can be made from the start.

The meeting should start with:

- an explanation of why it is being held
- a firm and agreed declaration of intent

leading to

- a discussion about why the coaching project is necessary
- the learner expressing the need to change or develop rather than this coming from the coach.

Specific content of the meeting

> Setting the plan
> Defining objectives
> Agreement on method
> The summary

Setting the plan

As soon as the need for remedial action or developmental coaching has been agreed, and the areas of need have been firmly identified, a plan of action can be formulated. This plan of action can only too easily be prescribed by the coach, but if the learner is to be fully committed to it and accept ownership of it, as far as possible it should be proposed by the learner. Prescription, guidance and advice by the coach, unless essential, should be at a minimum, and the coach will need to use every counselling skill available. In this context these skills include listening, questioning, probing, encouraging, seeking and bringing out ideas, exhibiting openness and trust, giving relevant information and feedback, and helping the learner to recognize their attitudes and feelings.

Ample time for discussion and planning should be made available at this stage to ensure that the learner realizes what is ahead and the extent of the trust being put in them.

Objectives

However simple and straightforward the coaching project might be, terminal objectives should not only be determined and agreed, but should be written down for both the coach and the learner. This objective statement should be simple and clear and can usefully follow the formula of: what, by whom, by when, in what manner, in what quantity and to what standards.

The key areas of the project should be defined critically so that, when the project is completed, a full and detailed discussion about what has been achieved is possible.

Time is another essential element, since if the learners are uncertain about how long they have to complete the project it will take either longer to perform than necessary or less time, and be done less effectively, because the learners will be so unsure about timing that they will rush the project. Time bounding also makes the project more real and relevant to work needs.

The coach should take care that the project is chosen not only because of work expediency, but also, or even *only* because of, the needs of the learner. A combination of these two factors is to be welcomed.

Agreement on the method

Again, the greater part of the suggestions for how the project should be conducted should originate with the learner rather than the coach. General approaches and some specific aspects should be agreed, but sufficient flexibility should be allowed to enable the learner to solve problems and decisions. The normal approach is for the coach to seek ideas from the learner, probe for clarification and development, build as necessary from the coach's experience, and seek alternative routes that the learner might take, rather than the one first thought of. Methods suggested by the learner that are known by the coach to lead to difficulties should not simply be rejected – the learner's actions in realizing and solving the problems are an integral part of their learning. Of course, in such circumstances the coach should keep a careful eye on progress and be ready to step in, in a relevant manner, if disaster seems unavoidable.

Optional methods for coaching will normally include:

> Learner's work review
> Selected higher level projects
> Training courses
> Open learning
> Multi-discipline approaches

Learner's work review

The simplest level of coaching will be for the coach to take a more significant interest and involvement in the work performed by the learner. On completion of a selected piece of work the coach and learner can meet to discuss it in terms of its success or otherwise, why it succeeded or failed, what methods were used, what other approaches could have been made to ensure success etc. This meeting should be conducted along the counselling lines suggested earlier.

Selected higher level projects

The coach could, at the next, higher level of coaching project, select one of their own simpler pieces of work for the learner to tackle, following a discussion similar to that described above. Before finalization of the project, the coach and learner would review progress and agree whether the project had been satisfactorily achieved, or agree additional steps to be taken.

The more complex level of coaching might include more difficult tasks belonging to the coach, or parts of one of these, parts for which the learner is given almost complete responsibility and authority.

Following a training course

Very few training courses are stand-alone events, so that when the learner returns to work arrangements must be made for them to practise their course learning and relate it to their working environment.

This post-course debriefing meeting should have been arranged before the learner attended the training event, and it should be held preferably in the week following the return of the learner. Items for discussion at this meeting will include:

> What the learner has learned
> What the learner intends to do with the learning
> Agreement on what is to be done
> Agreement on how it is to be implemented
> What supportive resources will be necessary
> What period of time is required/available
> How progress will be reviewed

The coach should also, separately, ensure that the learner's colleagues give support and that all the necessary resources are made available.

Following open learning

Use of these packages will almost certainly require some coaching support, possibly while the package is being studied (as problems or questions arise) and as an assessment of learning at the end of the study. In addition, the action recommended is the same as that following a training course, including discussion of needs for further open learning packages or other training approaches.

Multi-discipline approaches

This approach combines such techniques as open learning, training courses and the various coaching applications, and is a good example of the desirable co-operation between coach, manager, learner and trainer. All four people would be brought together in much closer collaboration than usual, so that the various aspects of the whole process can be linked effectively. Such a process might involve:

- the learner working through an open learning package, with interim support by the coach/manager
- an assessment by a training practitioner of the learning achieved at the end of the package, recommendations being made for further development, which may include attendance at a customized or relevant training course
- post-learning review and action planning between the learner and the manager/coach
- continuous review meetings between the coach and the learner, perhaps attended by the training practitioner for support and advice
- relevant additional coaching projects and attendance at training events.

The summary

The final part of the coaching meeting with the learner is a comprehensive review and summary of:

- what has to be done
- how it is to be done
- who will be involved
- when it will be completed.

Both coach and learner must be fully aware of what has been decided and share the same understanding. Because the overall approach in this coaching meeting is a counselling, rather than a prescriptive one, it is useful to invite the learner rather than the coach to produce the summary. This can have the effect of consolidating the details of the project in the mind of the learner, more than if the coach listed them. It also gives the coach the opportunity to check and amend any misunderstandings or omissions. It is also useful to write down the agreed summary – human memory is short, selective and capable of manipulation.

STAGE FIVE: AGREEMENTS FOR THE ASSIGNMENT REVIEWS AND THE FINAL REVIEW

Review procedures for the coaching project are so important that they are worth agreeing separately. Although the coach should not be 'looking over the shoulder' of the learner all the time, neither is it sufficient for the coach to arrange and start the process and then not take any further action until the end of the assignment – it may be too late by then. Consequently an important part of the process is the arrangement of reviews.

The number, extent, format and timing of the reviews will depend on the coaching task. In the case of a simple task only one interim review and a final review might be required, followed by further reviews based on the findings of the 'final' one as necessary. With more complex projects it is usually necessary to have a series of interim reviews to assess the progress of the project, modify agreements, suggest remedial action, discuss the resolution of problems etc. The number of these reviews will depend on the complexity of the project and the experience of the learner, but should be kept to a minimum.

The final review, arranged in accordance with the time bounding of the project, is the most important of all, and it must be scheduled.

STAGE SIX: IMPLEMENTATION

The reviews described above will be concurrent with the implementation of the project, but coaches must be reminded that they are not an opportunity to interfere in it. Interference (frequently unnecessary) is probably the main reason why learners lose interest in coaching, as they stop seeing it as an opportunity for *them* to grow. Once the project has started the coach should leave the learner alone to get on with it, until the agreed first review. This first review period is usually the shortest of the project, the actual period being determined by the complexity of the task and the experience of the learner. The agreements for the project should also include the advice to the learner that they can approach the coach at any time during the implementation, without waiting for a review, particularly if problems arise about which the learner is uncertain.

This is probably the most testing time for the coach, who will naturally be interested in (and perhaps a little uncertain about) how the learner and the task are progressing. The coach should follow two 'rules':

1. Leave the learner alone with the project, unless it becomes very obvious that something is going badly wrong.
2. Never take back a project simply because the learner is not progressing as fast as or in the way *you* would wish – there must be stronger reasons than this.

During the reviews

It is essential that the agreed reviews are held as arranged, as this will demonstrate continuing interest and support to the learner. The coach must not:

- say 'this is what you should do'
- provide unsolicited solutions to problems.

Rather they should try to bring the learner to their own conclusions and solutions by asking such questions as:

- What do you think you could do about it?
- What options are available to deal with this?
- How would you approach finding a possible solution to this problem?
- Have you thought about other possible solutions?
- Why do you feel that would be the most effective solution?
- What would you do if that solution didn't work?

During the review conflict and other negative reactions must be avoided and it helps not to use such emotive and discriminatory words as 'weakness', 'failing', 'failure' and 'poor'. In place of these, emphasis should be placed on successes and strengths, and where a lack of success has to be discussed it should be done in terms of improvement rather than rectification.

STAGE SEVEN: THE FINAL REVIEW

If the planning, project implementation and interim reviews have proceeded to plan, the coaching assignment will have been carried out successfully. But this will probably be only the start of a continuing process of coaching, with that individual or with others in the work unit. The event can now be one of further learning for the individual and for the coach.

As soon as possible after the end of the assignment a final review should be held between the learner and the coach. This meeting gives the coach the opportunity to review and discuss with the learner all that has happened, ensuring that praise is given if it is due. Equally, if the performance was less than what was intended, this should be discussed in an appropriate way. In theory, if the system of interim reviews has been performed effectively, failure should be minimal.

A useful start to the review is to seek the views of the learner as to how they felt the project had progressed. Shortfalls can be discussed and plans made to ensure that they would not recur. The reasons for success must also be questioned, so that any good practices learned might be used in other circumstances or a repeat of the project. The review will end, as far as the learner is concerned, with a restart of the cycle and action planning for the next stage of coaching.

But this is not the end for the coach. The project and the review of its achievements reflect not only how the learner has fared, but also the skill of the coach in planning, organizing, implementing and reviewing coaching. The coach, with feedback from the learner, can learn much by critically examining all aspects of the approach, in both areas that were successful as well as those that achieved less.

What next?

Few coaching assignments stand alone, certainly as far as the coach is concerned. As suggested above, the final review will not only be the occasion to consider the further coaching of the learner, but also time for consideration by the coach of what other coaching is necessary in the work unit.

There is no doubt that, if performed effectively and comprehensively, coaching is an expensive item in the coach/manager's time, particularly if there are a number of staff in the work unit – everybody has the right to some form of development. But coaching is only one of the manager's roles, and only a certain amount of time can be spent on it. This may be insufficient to satisfy the needs of all the staff. The solution lies in coaching itself. The busy manager can use some time effectively by coaching others in the techniques and skills of coaching, so that they in turn can coach others.

Coaching is not an easy option, but it has numerous long-term and lasting benefits for all concerned. Managed well it is less time consuming and difficult than is often imagined, but the time involved is amply repaid with widely skilled, motivated and efficient people, whose effectiveness will reflect well on the manager of the unit.

9
—

Delegating and Mentoring

This chapter:

- describes the barriers to and the benefits in people skills of the techniques of delegation
- discusses the most effective ways of carrying out delegation
- describes mentoring and gives guidance on how to introduce it as a possible skill.

DELEGATION

Delegation is frequently seen as a tactic used by managers and supervisors either to control the time management of their work or simply to get rid of the work that they cannot do, do not have time to do or do not want to do. But it can be a powerful tool in managing people skills and developing people and is often seen as part of the battery of techniques that can be included in the coaching process described in Chapters 7 and 8. It is often mistaken for other managerial tactics that do not add to the development of people, and descriptions of three approaches will help to place it in its correct perspective.

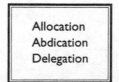

Allocation
Abdication
Delegation

Allocation. This is the straightforward distribution of work to members of a work unit, the tasks defining the job roles of those individuals, ie the normal work of the people of the unit. This enables the tasks of the unit to be performed but in no way enhances the skills of the individuals other than ensuring that they perform their work.

Abdication. This is when a manager 'allocates' some of the work for which he or she is personally responsible, simply to 'farm it out', and with no real aim of developing the recipients. This becomes even more obvious abdication when the manager takes no further interest in the allocated tasks, releasing all responsibility and authority.

Delegation. This, on the other hand, is when tasks or parts of a task that belong to the manager or supervisor are allocated to individuals in a structured and controlled way: (a) to enable the tasks to be performed and (b) to enable learning to take place. Like the wider aspects of coaching, delegation can be for remedial or developmental purposes, although the latter is usually the more common.

Barriers to delegation

At least eleven implied barriers to delegation can be identified:

1. It's my job to do all the work, after all I'm the manager/supervisor.
2. How do I know what to delegate?
3. By the time I've explained it, I could have done it myself.
4. How do I know it will be done correctly?
5. If I show them what to do, they'll be after my job.
6. It's too risky.
7. But I enjoy doing that myself!
8. I daren't just sit and think, I've got to be seen to be doing something.
9. I like to be on top of everything. If I delegate work I'll lose some of this contact.
10. They might do it better than me.
11. They might not like me giving them work.

It's my job to do all the work, after all I'm the manager/supervisor. It is not your job to do everything – management is the achievement of tasks through others. You will certainly have tasks that *must* be done by you personally, eg appraisal of 'your' staff, confidential staff reports etc, in addition to your supervision of certain areas of work. If you try to do more than this you will almost certainly fail in (a) the work for which you are immediately responsible and (b) the additional work you try to do. Also, you will be reducing the effectiveness of others, whom you are stopping performing new tasks. Delegation allows them to do their work *and* gives them the opportunity of developing more or higher level skills.

How do I know what to delegate? The simple answer is that, apart from the very personal tasks you must perform yourself, anything else could be delegated. Obviously this is not to be taken literally, principally because the people involved may have job duties to perform and could not accept the delegated tasks. But some tasks can be delegated to some people to further their development.

Examine your current tasks and prioritize them. Some may be large and complex tasks – break them down into smaller parts and perhaps distribute some of these among several members of staff, retaining some yourself. The delegated results can then be collated.

Even with some of the tasks that are unique to you, others can undertake parts of them, particularly if you train or coach them to do so.

If the people to whom you want to delegate work are fully occupied, it may be possible for them in their turn, with support and guidance from you, to delegate some of their work, giving them time to perform the delegated, developmental work.

By the time I've explained it, I could have done it myself. Naturally, but perhaps you haven't time to do it yourself, and this is the opportunity to help others to develop. It will take time, as neither you nor your staff are able to take on a new task *immediately*. Time taken to delegate correctly, involving discussion, coaching, training etc is expensive, but eventually you will save time as you will be able to delegate with ease and confidence, which allows you to get on with the jobs you *must* be doing. And you will have a capable, able, skilled, trained and developing staff.

How do I know it will be done correctly? If, in delegating tasks, you follow the guidelines given for coaching assignments – planning, setting up the task effectively, reviewing – you will be able to ensure that it is done correctly, without having always to be looking over the person's shoulder. The ultimate responsibility for the task is yours, but controlled delegation will ensure that any deficiencies or potential weaknesses are dealt with immediately so that there is less chance of failure.

If I show them what to do, they'll be after my job. Good! If this is what they are doing, they must be enthusiastic and motivated, and the best people to have working for you. With backing like this, if you share their feelings (which you have probably introduced and maintained), you will be progressing yourself. Someone in higher authority will notice the attitude, skill and effectiveness of your unit, kudos that will reflect on you. When you leave your post, you will do so with the satisfaction of knowing that you are leaving a successful team, the members of which you would have no hesitation in recommending or even taking with you.

It's too risky. If you give work to people who do not yet have the skill to perform it to 100 per cent efficiency, there is a risk that they will not make a success of it, but this is how people learn. Certainly any failure will rebound on you, but if the result is a resounding success, the consequent praise will also fall on you. Abdication will ensure failure, but effective delegation, where you ensure that: they know what they have to do; it is agreed how they will go about it; reviews and controls are built into the process will, if not ensuring success, avoid too significant a failure. Reviews will be held at identified critical points in the project and this will provide opportunities to remedy any deviations from the path of success. The ultimate responsibility lies with you, but by your taking appropriate delegatory action staff are more likely to succeed, they will understand their ownership of the action and their being given a share in the development.

But I enjoy doing that myself! But do you need to do it yourself? Some of our tasks are more enjoyable than others, but questions must be asked about their urgency and importance. Examine the jobs you tend to do first – almost certainly these will be the most enjoyable, the least difficult and the least important in your priority list. These are almost certainly the jobs you can delegate, leaving you the time to tackle the more challenging jobs. You can always hold back one or two of the 'enjoyable' jobs to give yourself a reward for hard work!

I daren't just sit and think, I've got to be seen to be doing something. Most tasks at a managerial level demand a significant amount of planning before implementation. This will involve a lot of thought, a period when it may appear that you are sitting doing nothing – in fact you are performing the most important part of the task. But many managers and supervisors fear – sometimes with justification in the culture of their organization – that if they seem to be doing nothing, it will be thought that they are not working.

If you feel that you have to 'justify' your thinking time, get into the habit, when planning, of having a pencil in your hand and making notes (even when you don't need to). Noting down your thoughts will in most cases help your thinking processes and will show that you are doing something.

Additionally, if as a result of your effective delegation and increased thinking time the results from your unit improve, let it be known how you obtained these results, and your actions will not be questioned.

I like to be on top of everything. If I delegate work I'll lose some of this contact. You are still ultimately responsible for the task you delegate and consequently must retain an interest in its progress. Your interim and final reviews will maintain required contact and the only contact with the work that you really lose will be with the details. Reviewing will in fact keep you more on top of a series of tasks than if you were trying to do them all yourself. You may feel threatened if you are asked about a particular (delegated) task and are unable to provide all the information immediately. The questioner should be made aware of the circumstances, and you can enhance the development of the person to whom the work was delegated by having them report progress themselves. You should be present at this reporting because:

- you will be updated on the progress of the task
- you can observe and appraise the presentation skills of the reporter
- your reporting subordinate will be encouraged to give reports (even though your presence may initially frighten them)
- your boss will be shown that you are an effective manager or supervisor with a capable staff in whom you have interest and confidence
- you are demonstrating to your team that you have confidence in them to take an active and independent, rather than a fully subordinate role.

Of course you will have to be careful during these reporting events, otherwise many of the points listed above can become negative indications. Your role should be that of observer and supporter, and you should intervene only if it becomes absolutely necessary. Even if the senior manager to whom the report is being given asks a question of you, this should be turned if appropriate to the reporter.

They might do it better than me. Nobody expects you to be a complete master of every task in your work unit, although you should have some knowledge of each of them and where to find relevant information. Current technology is demanding increasing specialism in ever narrower fields and some of your staff may be more highly qualified and skilled than you. Use these facilities and perhaps increase the number of important and demanding tasks you delegate. Your team will be encouraged by your recognition of their skills and your willingness to share and give them a greater variety of work.

They might not like me giving them work. Although this is a possibility it is unlikely if they realize why you are delegating and the benefits that accrue to them. Obviously a lot will depend on how you introduce and maintain the delegation. A useful activity is to hold a team meeting prior to starting on a programme of delegation to discuss the subject, describe your ideas and reach agreement.

You will almost certainly come across individuals who resent your trying to help them – they may see this as an attempt to make them work harder for no additional reward, or as a disciplinary act. They may be militant people who will automatically react against your ideas. Most of these resentments and rejections will be due to a misunderstanding about why you are delegating work. If you are unable to satisfy their doubts initially, you may find that as they see others developing through delegation they become more interested in being involved. Ensure that you are aware of this and repeat the opportunities for them to take part.

The principal impression you have to avoid giving is that you are offloading your own work for your own personal reasons – this will be seen as laziness on your part and an attempt to use staff for your own ends.

The benefits of delegation

So far the concentration has been on the barriers to delegation, barriers that you must certainly recognize, but in countering these, often mythical barriers, benefits have been seen to emerge. You will be:

- developing a more highly skilled, flexible team of people
- having more control of your own time
- able to concentrate on the tasks that demand the skills at your level
- able to have time to think and plan
- supported by a more skilled staff that will promote your image
- creating a committed, enthusiastic and effective team that will be easier to manage
- encouraged yourself by the development of other people
- using one of the most effective and cost-effective forms of training and development.

The benefits accrue not only to you and the organization, but also to the staff themselves, who will have:

- a greater variety of work
- the opportunity to learn and develop in natural surroundings
- a deeper and wider understanding of the work of the unit, your role and those of their colleagues
- the opportunity to demonstrate their abilities and potential
- increased flexibility in working methods
- obvious encouragement to be creative
- the opportunity to strengthen their relationships with the boss, their colleagues and other units
- the opportunity to influence others by their actions
- improved chances of promotion, or movement to more satisfying work, and/or greater earning power.

The process of delegation

The need for forethought and planning has been mentioned on several occasions and delegated work, rather than any other form of distribution, is planned and introduced with consideration for others. The process of delegation can be summarized as:

Considering tasks to delegate
Deciding who should do it and why
Meeting the delegatee
Implementation of the task
Final review and evaluation
Self-evaluation

Considering tasks to delegate. Every manager and supervisor has at any one time a variety of work tasks, and when considering delegation must decide:

- which ones they are going to retain to do themselves
- which ones can be allocated
- which ones can be delegated.

When the decision is made to allocate or delegate the tasks should be selected very carefully, particularly those to be delegated. Remember delegation is not a means of avoiding the jobs you do not enjoy doing!

Deciding who should do it and why. Delegation can be carried out to:

- relieve your own work load
- improve the performance of the poorer worker
- develop the knowledge and skills of an already effective person.

In the first case you will probably need to identify the people who already have most of the skills needed to perform the particular task at the right level.

The other two cases will involve you in the most preparation and action: planning to delegate; counselling and discussion; reviewing during the task; substantial post-task review. It may be necessary to break the tasks down into more manageable bits for the delegatee or to spread a complex task over several people.

The third case differs from the second in that it will probably require less planning and meeting time because the individuals are more likely to be more capable and motivated than poorer performers. Less review time will also be required, but it is necessary to ensure that sufficient review time is given to assess and plan development.

Meeting the delegatee. The worst possible introduction to delegation for the person concerned is for notification to be given in a note or by third person word of mouth. Meeting the delegatee is a very important part of the process and frequently determines the success or otherwise of the delegation. The aim of this meeting is *agreement*, not *prescription*. Newcomers to delegation will benefit from following a logical pattern for this meeting.

1. Agree with the person that they are willing to take on tasks with which they are not familiar and which may be more difficult than their normal work. This may be more of a problem when the person is a poorer performer rather than one ripe for development. The former may be suspicious of your motives or nervous about taking on more responsibility. You must ensure that these fears are allayed before proceeding with the delegation.
2. Describe the task fully in terms of:
   - who owns the task, ie responsibility for the task and who requires its completion
   - exactly what is involved in the task implementation
   - the objectives of the exercise – the training and development of the person to improve their knowledge, skills and job satisfaction
   - any constraints on its performance
   - what authority is given for necessary resources, materials, people support
   - the completion deadline
   - how the task will be seen to be successful.

3. Ensure, either by summarizing or asking the delegatee to summarize the information about the project and what has been discussed, that they have full understanding of the delegated task.

4. Discuss and agree with, don't *tell*, the delegatee how the task could be performed most effectively. *Only* if their proposed method would lead to certain failure should you disagree directly; otherwise ask the delegatee for alternative suggestions to compare and select the most appropriate.

5. Discuss and agree any training necessary to help the delegatee to perform the task more effectively.

6. Discuss and agree any dates for progress reviews, the complexity of the task, what it involves and the skill of the delegatee should determine the number and frequency of these reviews.

7. Agree or, as relevant, state the deadline date and arrange a review before this date to allow for additional or remedial action.

8. Agree a final review date to assess the completed task, discuss learning achieved and future action.

Implementation of the task. Implementation is in the hands of the delegatee, and the manager should not only take a back seat but should avoid interrupting or interfering, apart from at review times, and then only under the strict terms of the review. Obviously intervention becomes necessary if it is seen that failure is likely, but these occasions should be few and far between in a well-organized delegation. In some ways, even worse than actually intervening is for the manager to *hover* while the person is performing the task – breathing down people's necks is a certain way to unsettle them and jeopardize the task performance.

However, the worst action the delegator can take is to stop the person performing the task and take it back, usually because it is felt that the delegatee is not implementing the task effectively. This must be an absolutely last resort. The delegatee might come and appear ready to give up because they feel stuck, cannot understand a point or feel incapable of finishing the task. It is then only too easy to take back the task and finish it yourself. This should be resisted and a counselling discussion, rather like the starting discussion, initiated to resolve the problems and allow the delegatee to continue.

Final review and evaluation. As suggested earlier, this should take place sufficiently before the end of the delegated task for any problems or errors to be remedied. The final success of the project should be assessable at this meeting and the delegatee given the go-ahead to complete the task. If the project has been set up correctly, and effectively controlled through reviews, this final review should rarely be traumatic.

A further, *evaluative* review can be held once the task has been completed. At this review the discussion can centre around the learning that the person has attained from the project, how they can implement that learning in other areas, and what can happen next to develop the person – training, further delegated tasks, a programme of coaching, open learning etc. Notice must be taken of what the delegatee feels and wants, linked with (hopefully the same) what the manager feels that they need. These must be acted upon, otherwise all the benefits of the delegation will be lost, not only for that individual but also for others, who will note what has happened and may go off the idea of performing delegated tasks.

The main topics that should be considered in this review include:

- How well did the delegated task go?
- What were the major influences on the extent and level of its progress?
- What problems did the delegatee find in the task and process?
- What did the person learn from the event?
- How can this learning be used in the future?
- Does the person want to take on other delegated tasks? If so, of what nature?
- What form should an action plan for the future take?

Self-evaluation. Delegation can be a learning instrument for the manager as well as the learner, particularly if the manager plans to continue a programme of delegation. He or she should take some time to consider:

What has the delegation done for you?

What have you learned about delegation?

What have you learned about the person involved?

What else have you learned?

Would you repeat the process? If so, with what changes?

Did it save you time?

If so, what did you do with that time?

How can you further improve your delegation techniques?

MENTORING

Mentoring can be considered a broader version of coaching and delegation, usually introduced for the training and development of new entrants to the industry, the organization or a particular unit of work. The traditional approach to a new entrant is frequently GAFO – go away and find out. Mentoring formalizes this approach and gives the newcomers support in their early period of discovery. In its simplest form mentoring is the nomination of a person or persons in the same work unit as the newcomer who is advised to approach these people if they have any questions or problems. At its most complex mentoring can involve a new or trainee manager with a senior manager who is nominated as the mentor and who effects a full developmental programme, supported by other managers, experts and training practitioners.

Mentoring can be considered in terms of:

> Who mentors?
> What is done?
> How is it done?
> Directive
> Non-directive
> Supportive

Who mentors?

The mentor will usually be an existing member of the organization drawn from the ranks of senior managers, line managers, training practitioners and, where relevant, experts or specialists in discrete work areas. The mentor is usually also an older person with a wide experience and knowledge of the job or organization. Criteria for an appropriate mentor would include:

- a genuine interest in helping younger or less experienced people
- no jealousy of or fear for their own position
- a wide knowledge of learning approaches, but not necessarily training techniques
- ability to create empathy with the learner
- the backing of the organization so that all necessary resources are available, as well as time to practise the mentoring effectively.

Mentor attributes

A more detailed and comprehensive list of attributes would extend the above to include the following:

1. *Relating to the organization*
   - knows the organization – products, hierarchy, plans, vision and culture
   - has a good appreciation of the job the learner is performing and where they might be heading in the organization
   - has a vision of the future of the organization
   - knows the organization's career and progress structure and methods
   - is well regarded personally throughout the organization.
2. *Empathy and understanding*
   - has a genuine interest in developing others
   - can relate to problems found by inexperienced people
   - neither jealously guards own position nor is defensive in sharing knowledge and skills
   - wants people to learn and perform well
   - can command respect by personality, behaviour and skills rather than by position
   - is willing to react to learner requirements at unstructured and sometimes inconvenient times.
3. *Training skills*
   - can organize a learning process
   - can personally train/teach/instruct when necessary
   - has good counselling skills and can help others identify their own needs and methods of fulfilling them
   - can identify when and how to pose questions, particularly probes
   - can concentrate on asking the appropriate questions rather than give information or prescriptions
   - has an understanding of learning styles, barriers and motivations and can utilize this knowledge
   - has an understanding of and skills in using a number of training methods
   - can communicate facts, information, feelings, views and emotions fully and accurately
   - has good influencing skills, particularly with peers and more senior managers.

4. *Time*
   - has been allocated time by the organization to fulfil the demands and needs of the learner
   - is a good personal time manager
   - devotes the required time to the mentoring function.

What is done?

The mentoring practice will depend on the approach determined, the level of the mentor and mentored, whether the mentoring is to be formal or informal, ie in an unstructured or structured way. A mentor can fulfil this role often without realizing it – many chief executives, managing directors, other captains of industry etc admit that people in the industries they entered have helped them, whether as idols, father figures or direct practical supporters. However, in the more formal field of training and development, mentors usually have specific roles and functions.

How is it done?

There are three main forms of mentoring in industry: directive, non-directive and supportive, each demanding different approaches and techniques.

Directive mentoring

In general this approach is the most effective when the person to be mentored is completely new to work, to the organization and/or to the job. It is also more frequently used for less senior posts in which the work is very well defined and structured and contained to a large extent within procedures and systems.

The role demands very strong people skills and tact in allocating and controlling learning tasks without being too obtrusive and without making the learners feel they are being directed. A great deal of time will be necessary as the mentor becomes almost a personal trainer. In this approach the mentor:

- decides which activities the learner should follow
- plans and designs the mentoring programme and the time required
- tells the learner what is needed
- acts as the trainer, instructor or coach
- evaluates task achievement in the learner

- sells ideas for progression
- reflects the superior/subordinate relationship.

Non-directive mentoring

This is directly the reverse of directive mentoring and requires the mentor to avoid over-direction while ensuring that the learner is aware of how to obtain information and/or help. An approach using non-directive mentoring might be to let the learner know exactly what they are required to do, in general terms, and place the onus on the learner to progress their learning. A mentor is appointed and briefed to help the learner whenever they are approached for guidance and advice. The learner is given the name and location of their mentor and told that it is that person who should be contacted if they require any information, guidance, advice or help. The specific activities of the mentor then include:

- avoiding giving advice unless this is specifically sought
- allowing the learners to determine their own learning direction and planning
- encouraging reflection and analysis on the part of the learner
- being available when required by the learner.

The non-directive approach will be most useful (and easier to practise) with learners who have substantial experience in the organization or industry and in self-directed learning. Obviously they will need to be highly motivated to learn, know how to go about this, but willing to admit ignorance of some areas and also to seek help.

Supportive mentoring

This is a compromise approach between the other two and takes features from both.

The supportive mentor is available when contacted by the learner, but also takes proactive action. This does not mean prescribing for the learner, but involves discussion, counselling, encouraging and agreeing courses of action. The activities of a supportive mentor include:

- facilitating the learner's progress
- performing direct training where required
- counselling the learners on their learning and training needs
- helping the learner prepare a plan of action
- allowing the learner as far as possible to decide on their own actions, but being ready to intervene if the approach is going wrong

- intervening in a questioning rather than directive mode
- being willing to take the blame for failure of the process
- not claiming credit for success (this will be unnecessary as the success will be evident!).

A mentoring format

The actual format and content will depend on the nature of the learning, the skill and experience of the learner and the behaviour pattern of the mentor. A typical supportive mentoring process might ensue from the following description.

1. *Allocation of a mentor*. The mentor would be selected by the organization (frequently the training and development department who would have overall responsibility for making the most suitable arrangements) from the appropriate level – a peer operative at the production level to a senior manager at, say, the graduate management trainee level. The ideal person would be older than the learner, but not too much older, to make the age gap very evident or to be unable to relate to the learner.
2. *Initial discussion*. The first contact between the learner and the mentor, following perhaps an informal introductory meeting, would be a discussion during which:
   - the two participants can begin to get to know each other, their attitudes, behaviours, needs and objectives
   - the ground rules for the mentoring process are agreed
   - the final objectives for the learner are agreed
   - plans for where, how and when the objectives might be achieved are agreed
   - the role of the mentor is defined and agreed
   - interim reviews and a final review discussion are agreed, the latter on a provisional basis.
3. *Initial activities*. More specific learning activities could be an initial shadowing of the mentor by the learner. He or she would sit with the mentor while that person works: approaching problems; making decisions; communication face to face, on the telephone and in writing; preparing for and attending meetings and so on. All working activities would be observed, (with the exception perhaps of personal counselling or appraisal of staff) and discussed.
4. *Subsequent activities*. These can take many forms and could include:
   - direct training by the mentor
   - attendance by the learner on training events

- open learning packages, supported by the mentor
- assignment of projects
- secondments or attachments to various departments or job functions
- discussions with heads of other departments or specialists in discrete functions
- coaching programmes.

Many of the learner's activities should be real projects, utilizing actual work, and selected to give the learner the widest possible view of the organization, its work and the types of involvement the learner might expect in the future. Whether the mentor is directly involved or not with each of the learner's projects, there must be continuous contact and review.

5. *Mentoring report*. The final action in the mentoring process will be the completion of a report for the learner's sponsors – senior management, the training department, the appropriate line manager – on the achievements of the mentoring. Ideally this report will be prepared as a joint project by the mentor and learner – a further learning experience – and can include the views of both.

Mentoring is far from being an easy option, as it can be time consuming and expensive, but it has considerable value and can be very effective.

10

Role Plays

This chapter:

- considers the different types of one-to-one interaction training and the training approaches employed
- details the techniques used in role playing in training and development
- reviews the methods that can be used to observe, review and feedback role play interactions.

A role play is a training situation in which two or more learners take the parts of characters other than themselves and act out the situation with which they have been presented.

THE VALUE OF ROLE PLAYS

The majority of our interactions with other people occur in a one-to-one, face-to-face environment, whether these are informal, conversational meetings, or more formal, focused discussions. It is most often in these type of interactions that relations between the people involved fall down, and any training and development that can decrease the chances of these failures is to be welcomed. As in obtaining skills and experience in most people behavioural situations, the techniques and methods of role play can be learned from books, videos, open learning packages etc, but the real learning can come about only through live practice and experience. Practice is available on training courses and these have a further advantage, one not usually available in real-life situations, in the provision of feedback by the trainer, the other person in the interview and any observers present.

TYPES OF ONE-TO-ONE INTERACTION TRAINING

Role plays usually take place in one-to-one interaction training events and generally involve some form of interview training, in which both the appropriate techniques and the behaviours are considered. These events are commonly concerned with:

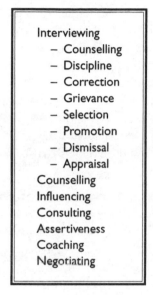

Interviewing
- Counselling
- Discipline
- Correction
- Grievance
- Selection
- Promotion
- Dismissal
- Appraisal
Counselling
Influencing
Consulting
Assertiveness
Coaching
Negotiating

TRAINING APPROACHES

In training for the types of interaction listed above there are many similarities of approach, certainly on the behavioural side, each type requiring some differences in the procedure or techniques. Perhaps the most common training approach for this area follows a pattern of:

- ■ A small group (about 12 people) training event
- ■ Learning concerned with the specific technique(s) of people interaction, including questioning methods
- ■ Practice of the techniques in observed pairs
- ■ Feedback of the observed interactions
- ■ Behaviour awareness and modification

Group learning

Although the use of group training is not essential in people interaction training, it has advantages, in that a number of people can learn at the same time, be advised and guided in a common manner, have the opportunity to practise interviewing with a number of people, and receive feedback from a number of sources. The group operates as a full group usually only when inputs are being given on techniques and when other discussions are being held that require the input of a number of opinions. The rest of the time the group is divided into interviewing pairs accompanied by an observer from the group. In this way a number of face-to-face interviews can be held at the same time and, as a result, more practice interviews can be held with the participants being mixed to provide as much different contact as possible.

The structure of this type of event also provides an opportunity, not only for maximum feedback, but also for a variety of feedback approaches. This subject will be described fully later in this chapter.

Specific technique learning

Apart from general behaviour awareness and modification training, one-to-one interaction training involving role plays is usually concerned with a specific form of interaction. These were listed earlier, and while some have their own particular techniques and approaches the majority have common approaches.

For example, counselling techniques usually require the counsellor (the learner acting as the counsellor in training situations) to create an empathic environment, ask questions principally of an open and reflective nature, and generally encourage the interviewee to do the talking. Relevant information is given by the counsellor when sought, or offered if it is sufficiently important and the interviewee does not appear aware of its existence (and therefore cannot ask about it). The principal role of the counsellor is listening and leading the interviewee to understand their own feelings and position and come to their own decisions.

This description can be applied to many interview situations in which we find ourselves when dealing with people, and are the basic people skills. The description can certainly be applied directly to recruitment, grievance and promotion interactions, the remainder differing only slightly. For example, in the case of the disciplinary or correction interview, the interviewer would introduce the subject, rather than the interviewee, by detailing the error or omission. But then the interview would take on more of a counselling nature, with the interviewer seeking the views and information from the interviewee. A formal disciplinary interview would close with the interviewer detailing the sanctions to be taken, although there would still be a counselling aspect to try to have the offender agree to change, rather than simply prescribing that they had to change.

Similarly with appraisal interviews when, after any statutory statement about the interviewee's performance, the nature of the interview changes to a futuristic discussion in which the individual mainly suggests action to be taken.

Training events concerned with negotiation are rather different from the remainder as they have a substantial number of specific techniques and approaches. But the training approach using role plays is very similar to that used in interview situations.

Whatever the nature of the interaction in question, or the differences between types of interaction, the training event will usually start with some form of input or discussion of the techniques involved, preferably on an interactive basis. This will be particularly important with a group of learners who are new to the techniques and approaches. With learners who already have some skill, the initial stages will be more biased to discussion and experience sharing than to 'instruction'.

Practice of the techniques in observed pairs

The next stage will usually be practice of the techniques and approaches described. Initial role plays in an event might be simple ones, not based on the subject itself, but more general, such as asking the group, in pairs, to interview each other about their views on soccer violence, the role of the monarchy etc. The purposes of these initial interviews is to accustom the participants to talking to each other and probing for views and information, prior to taking part in more specific interview subjects.

The role plays in most of these cases will consist of two participants, the interviewer (perhaps as counsellor or role playing manager), and the interviewee (perhaps a member of staff or someone with a problem). A third participant can be a fellow group member who will act as observer of the interaction, making notes of the process and the behaviours, so that feedback can be given after the event. The role play can be a 'real' interaction, a constructed case study, or one based on an issue suggested by the group members. Each have their advantages and disadvantages and the choice will be based on the type of event, the nature of the subject, the existing skill of the learners and their willingness to take open parts in the event.

One of the general problems experienced in training events using a number of role plays, with the intention of giving the learners as much practice as possible, is the risk that by the third practice interview the learners are becoming bored with the repetitive process. The way to combat this is to vary the event. 'Real' interactions can be mixed with constructed role plays, the third person can be omitted and the participants required to observe and feedback themselves, or the full group invited to develop a structure for the interaction then practise *their* structure, and so on. Additionally some of the special forms of role play, described later, can be used instead of the straight role play.

Feedback of the observed interactions

There are several methods by which role plays can be observed and feedback given to the participants, but whichever method is used it is essential that some form of feedback is given. Without this the participants have only their own observations on which to rely, and these can be distorted, not only by a false internal view of what they are doing, but by their being so immersed in the activity that critical incidents, perhaps noted at the time, can be forgotten by the time the interaction comes to an end.

As we shall see later, the method of observation and feedback used can be selected from a number of approaches – the trainer alone, the trainer supported by a learner, a single learner colleague, several learner colleague observers, video observation and group feedback, video recording and self-discovery feedback (perhaps supplemented by direct feedback), full group direct observation followed by a feedback discussion etc.

Behaviour awareness and modification

The procedures, techniques and approaches are important in trying to produce a successful interaction, but equally important, and perhaps more so, are the behaviours used with the more technical processes. Awareness of the behaviours exhibited can be treated generally, or, preferably, in a specific way with the use of an instrument such as Behaviour Analysis to record the observed behaviours. These can then be analysed so that any necessary modifications can be identified and used in the subsequent interaction practices. The use of such an instrument will largely depend on the time available for description and practice of the process, and it may be that the trainer alone may have to use BA and feed back the results to the learners. This may be problematical when parallel-running practice interviews with only one trainer available are used, and if time is not available to train the learners then observation and subsequent feedback may be forced back to simple, general behavioural observation.

THE NATURE OF ROLE PLAYS

A variety of types of role plays and techniques for using them are available, including:

> Constructed role plays
> Constructions from real situations
> Real situations

Special techniques can include:

> Triads
> Role doubling
> Role reversal
> Empty chair
> Psychodrama
> Hot role plays

Constructed role plays

In most cases role plays are simulated situations that have been constructed by the trainer to enable a range of learning points to be practised. For example, in a discipline interviewing event, one individual in each pair might take the part of the manager, using a prepared incident brief to enable him or her to start the interview. The brief might include short details of the person to be interviewed, what has been reported that has led to the discipline need and the sanctions available. The other person, the interviewee, will be given a similar brief, slanted towards the offender's viewpoint with perhaps additional information about which the manager knows nothing.

The briefs will include observation of all the techniques used, comparing their actual use with the discussion in the preceding learning section. The behaviours to be used in such an interaction would also have been identified and would need to be looked for during the event.

The principal advantages of a role play of this type are that each pair can be given the same situation, in which the role play constructor knows there are several critical incidents that require the use of particular techniques and behaviours. The role play can be tailored to the skill or experience of the learners or to situations with which they will be familiar and the result is a controlled, learning event.

The disadvantages include the artificiality of both the case study used in the role play and the need for the learners to take on roles that may be alien to them. The construction of an 'artificial' role play, however closely it might be based on a real situation, exaggerates the problem. Carefully constructed briefs have to be produced for the 'interviewer' and the 'interviewee', which must be sufficiently detailed to give the learners ample material on which to base their role playing, yet sufficiently short for them to remember the case without constant reference to the brief during the interaction. This requires a careful balance. It is not uncommon for learners to blame their 'failure' on deficiencies in the brief or the amount of data they had to remember. The other excuse is wider and is based on the learners' views that 'of course, we wouldn't do this in real life, back at work!'.

These two disadvantages can be somewhat reduced by:

1. ensuring that the brief is of optimum length, clear, comprehensive yet concise, and that ample time is given to the learners to study the brief before they have to role play
2. basing the role play on real-life incidents, tailored as far as possible to the specific learning group.

A more difficult problem to combat is that, even with all the conditions for effective role plays being satisfied, the participants have to 'act' to varying degrees. Some people are natural actors in role plays, others find it difficult but cope, and yet others claim they are unable to act. The real-life role play (described later) may appear to satisfy this objection. But there are some people who, although capable and efficient at work, performing almost exactly the same requirement, are unable to do so in a training environment, particularly in front of others and knowing that they are to be assessed. In the most extreme cases the impossibility of role playing has to be accepted and these learners can often be utilized as observers.

Constructed role plays from real situations

Comments have already been made about the benefits of a role play constructed from a real-life situation, preferably one with which the learners are familiar, and this is strongly recommended. A construction that is often even better than this is to seek descriptions of case studies from within the learning group itself – there then can be little room for excuses that the role play is not real. The 'owners' of the cases can be asked to produce briefs for the role plays, which is one way to avoid criticism of unhelpful briefs produced by the trainer! Although it may sometimes defeat the usefulness of a known case study there can be value in giving learners other than the 'owner' the case study to role play. The 'owner' can be valuable in the review and feedback, particularly comparing what actually happened with the approaches used in the role plays, but they should not denigrate the role play results (which can on occasions be more appropriate than what actually happened!).

Real situations

These differ from the constructed role plays in that situations occurring on the training event itself are used as role play events. A wide variety can be used, ranging from the pairs being asked to interview each other about issues that have arisen from the training, to counselling set-ups, when some of the participants have problems they would like to talk through, to the resolution in a controlled interview of a conflict situation that has arisen. The latter can become what is known as a 'hot role play' – see pages 148–9.

SOME SPECIAL ROLE PLAY TECHNIQUES

Role doubling

Role doubling or ghosting describes the situation when participants other than the original role players take part in the interaction, although not necessarily taking over the interaction. The switch of active role players has to be performed carefully and, if it is to occur on more than one occasion, special care must be taken that the original role players are not upset. If the learners, although wanting to practise this technique, are inexperienced or unskilled, the trainer might be the role doubler in the initial stages, demonstrating the technique.

Role doubling is normally used during a conventional role play interaction between two participants who have agreed to carry out the role play in front of some of the remainder of the group. Role doubling will have been described and acceptance given for its use on relevant occasions.

A typical case might be when, during the course of, say, a problem-solving interview, the participant – manager or problem owner – has to suggest possible solutions. It may become obvious that the participants are in trouble and there is a danger of the interaction failing. At this stage, the 'ghost', who has a suggestion to offer, goes and stands behind the participant for whom they want to double and, speaking as that person in the environment of the interaction, makes the suggestion. The other participant can then react to this, perhaps raising a question which might be responded to by the original role player, if they are ready to re-enter the interaction. If this happens, the ghost returns to their seat and the interaction continues. If the original participant is still not ready, the ghost can continue until the original person is prepared to do so and the interview can progress smoothly.

One of the principal problems with other learners intervening is the reaction of the original participant, who might (a) simply resent the intervention or (b) resent it because they were not stuck and were considering their response. The trainer should be skilled at interventions of this nature, but on occasions other learners might want to act as the role double – frequently the trainer can observe this through the body language of the person who wants to intervene. The intervention can then be stopped or allowed.

I have had experience of learners who did not intervene or were not interrupted as the participant saying that if it had happened to them they would have resented the intrusion. However, if questioned, most participants who are ghosted report in the review session that they welcomed the support as they had been completely lost and they learned a lot from the way the interview continued.

A rather different form of role doubling can help the learning achieved in role plays. Before an interview starts, agreement can be reached that, at stages (perhaps indicated by the trainer as the interaction proceeds), a pattern of doubling will take place. This gives a larger number of people the opportunity to take part in an interaction and also allows them to try out ideas they might have had while they were waiting their turn. This arrangement can also be of help to learners who would be too shy to intervene voluntarily.

Role reversal

This is a more novel method of using a real-life case study as a role play. The traditional approach would be to set up a role play situation with the problem 'owner' taking their original part in the interaction and another, well-briefed, participant taking the other person's part. This has the advantage of giving the problem owner the opportunity to try a different approach to assess which one might have produced a better result, or to repeat the original case and seek feedback of the views of others on how the case was handled. The way we approach a problem can often blind us to other ways of handling it and we commonly hear the statement 'If he could only see the problem from my point of view!' Role reversal attempts to achieve this.

The role play can start off normally, with the problem owner taking the real-life part, but at a crucial point in the interaction the trainer stops the event and requires the two participants to reverse roles. Being forced to take the other person's part, and therefore attitude, the problem owner has to argue from a completely different viewpoint and can begin to see the problem from the other's point of view. This is not an easy technique and usually requires a considerable amount of information and attitude briefing for the other person. The ideal, of course, would be to repeat the case, under the controlled conditions of the training event, with both real participants.

The empty chair or monodrama

This technique stems from psychological practice and is used to take the pressure off someone who wants to give vent to their feelings. One of the problems encountered in traditional role playing is that, even if the problem owner takes one of the roles, the other person has to act a role for which the brief may not be all encompassing. The empty chair approach allays the need for a second person in the fundamental process of helping the problem owner to face the problem.

The basic approach is for the problem owner to sit with an empty chair facing them. The participant is encouraged to start talking about the problem to the empty chair as if a sympathetic listener was sitting there – frequently the trainer needs to help in guiding the participant in the early stages, but usually the trainer can soon withdraw as the person becomes more at ease with the event. Because there is no possibility of interruption the problem owner can fully develop the argument or case and frequently a participant becomes so involved in the monologue that the absence of a real listener is forgotten. Possible solutions can be proposed and discussed and hopefully conclusions reached. At the very least, the problem owner has been given a full opportunity to verbalize the problem without the added complication of other people and the roles they might play.

A variation that demands rather more activity and mental agility involves the switching of the problem owner between the two chairs. Once the basic statement of the problem has been made to the empty chair, and some aspects developed, the participant moves to the 'empty chair' and takes on the role of another person, asking questions, raising objections or making suggestions as if they were the other, participant in an interaction. The problem owner then switches back to the original chair and answers the objections etc, before moving back again to the 'empty' chair to continue the 'discussion'. The alternate switching of chair positions continues until the problem has been talked through successfully. Often, after some switching, the problem owner stays in the original position and, in a straight monologue, simply talks through and concludes the problem.

Psychodrama

This is an extension of the empty chair technique and can be used when the problem is causing highly emotional feelings that need release. The approach is to encourage the person to relive the bad feelings and experience. The line between training and therapy in this case is very thin and extreme care has to be taken psychodrama that even more damage is not caused. The trainer will have to guide the participant in the early stages by encouraging and helping in the process of letting the problem emerge, but should quickly withdraw and allow the problem owner to proceed how and as far as they wish. A trainer using this technique should be skilled not only in training techniques and very aware of behaviour signalling, but also in therapeutic counselling skills, as high emotions can be generated. However, at its simplest it is a very powerful technique that allows people to express themselves freely and release feelings that might otherwise be bottled up.

Hot role plays

These were mentioned earlier when real-life role plays were being discussed. An extension of the real situation is to use 'here and now' events to provide the material for interactions. As with psychodrama, extreme care must be taken, particularly if the issues being raised are highly emotionally charged. A hot role play can, for example, come about from the disagreement between two people on the training course, and the event is acted out to (a) give the people concerned the opportunity to practise real interpersonal people skills and (b) solve the problem, or at least give it a therapeutic airing.

Little setting up is required for an event of this nature, other than having the participants agree to take part in the interaction, perhaps in front of the remainder of the training group. Situations in which the hot role play can be used might be when two people disagree about the use and value of a practice that has been introduced on the course, where there may be a misunderstanding between the two which has resulted in bad feelings, where something has been said that is impeding the interactive process for the two people and so on.

If, as is preferable for learning purposes, the interaction is staged before the remainder of the group (full agreement must be obtained from the two participants for this) the early stages can be difficult, slow and even painful until the participants warm to the opportunity of settling their differences using their people skills. Again with the permission of the two players, the group might become involved in the process, particularly if difficulties are being experienced and the observers can see ways out, ways that are hard to see from the inside. In such cases the event becomes almost a 'family' counselling situation and can increase the cohesiveness of the group.

OBSERVATION AND FEEDBACK

Observation

However valuable the release of feelings and the practice of interaction skills might be in role plays, the development of skill is incomplete without an assessment of and feedback on how the participants have executed the interactions. The first step is one of observation of the interactions by external observers, who can give the participants feedback on their actions and behaviour.

The methods and instruments for observing a variety of situations were described and illustrated in Chapters 5 and 6, including the use of Behaviour Analysis in observing one-to-one people interactions. Many of these can also be used in observing role plays, and the practical choices generally fall between:

- observation by the trainer alone
- observation by both the trainer and the course members
- observation by fellow course members.

Linked with these approaches are decisions about whether:

- an instrument, such as BA, or general observational techniques should be used
- the observations should be made in the room with the participants
- there should be indirect observation by means of closed circuit television.

Trainer/trainer and member/member observation

Although the trainer is probably the most skilled and experienced observer, only one viewpoint and voice is represented and their non-member position in the group might reduce the acceptability of their views. However, in spite of this, the trainer is frequently called upon to give a definitive identification or interpretation of an event.

At the other end of the spectrum, observation and feedback by the participants' fellow course members is usually acceptable although if, as is normally the case, only one peer observer is used, they are in the position of the trainer in being only one voice. Also it is not unusual for participants, although willing to accept their fellows' comments, to question whether they have the skill to really observe the critical aspects of the interaction.

An apparent compromise would be for the trainer to observe in company with a peer observer. This also presents problems, in that with multi- and parallel use of practice role plays the trainer can only assist with one role play interaction.

The most acceptable and practical compromise is for each pair of participants to have a fellow course member as their observer, as in a Triad, but a considerable amount of preparation is essential. The observers must be well drilled in what they have to look for – process and behaviour, and how they are to do this – using a general observation instrument or a BA form. This suggests that early in a people skills training course time should be given to enable all the group members to learn at least some of these skills – 'all' because the intention should be for every course member to act as an observer and a role play participant on at least one occasion during the event.

The observers must also be fully aware of all 'public' aspects of both sides of the role play. The observers should be given copies of both briefs before the role play practice and given time to study these; this can take place at the same time that the participants are studying their briefs. As suggested in Chapter 6, the observer 'group' might also be given the opportunity to plan their observations and perhaps design their own observational sheets.

Direct or indirect observation

Live and direct observation can take several forms, the one used depending on the way the role plays are set up. If there is to be one practice interview by two participants in front of the remainder of the group, this remainder will all act as observers. This is not a recommended approach as considerable pressure is placed on the participants, feedback can become difficult to control, and it suggests that the amount of practice will be limited.

The more usual format when multi-practice pairs are used is for the role play participants to be accompanied by a fellow course member who acts as observer. This observer should sit away from the two participants and be as unobtrusive as possible, making notes as agreed as the interaction proceeds.

Such direct observation has the advantage that the observer is personal to the two participants, is known to be observing them, and is in the same position as they are – he or she is a fellow course member and will be observed in turn when further practices take place.

Disadvantages include:

■ the observers' criticism might be tempered by the thought that they themselves will eventually be observed
■ as course members, they may not be skilled or experienced in observing people
■ their presence in the room may be seen as obtrusive.

Closed circuit television (CCTV). The replacement of a human, direct observer by a CCTV camera in the interview practice room counteracts the criticism of an obtrusive observer. However, the human observer has simply been replaced by an inanimate object, the spy in the corner. Some people will react even more strongly against the camera than against a fellow, human observer (see pages 88–90). Human observation is still recommended with CCTV, but in this case the observer will be watching the monitor and making their observation notes. Bearing in mind the problems created by making the camera obtrusive, close-ups of one participant can be obtained or both people included in the same shot, aiding the recognition and recording of slight body signals.

One major advantage that CCTV has over human observation is that the interaction can be recorded and played back after the interview. The participants might argue over incidents with a human observer, but the video recording gives absolute proof of what happened.

Feedback

Whichever method of observation is used, it must be remembered that its principal purpose is to give critical feedback to the participants on their use of the relevant techniques and their people behaviour. If this is not to be given (usually for reasons of time, as feedback can take longer than the event) no observation should be undertaken other than reliance on the observational capabilities of the participants themselves.

Use of peer observers

If human observers are used, either as direct observers within the practice room or at the end of the CCTV link, two principal feedback processes are possible.

1. When the interactions are complete and some time has been given for the participants to move from their roles back to reality, and for the observers to finalize their notes, all the participants and the observers return to the training room. Feedback then takes place with the full group, each observer commenting on their own interaction followed by a general discussion on emergent principles and practices.
2. When the interactions are complete the participants and observer stay together and feedback takes place in each small group. This is followed by a full group discussion on significant issues that have emerged, or lessons to be drawn.

Whichever is used, a useful formula for following feedback can be:

1. The principal participant, for example the 'manager', is asked how he or she felt they had performed in the interview.
2. The other participant is then asked (a) how they felt they had performed or responded during the interview and (b) what feelings they had about the actions and behaviour of the interviewer.

Both these comments can be guided by seeking good points in the process, weaker points, what they could have done better, whether the other person helped or hindered the process.

3. The observers can then add their comments, if the two participants have not already made them, correct any 'mistakes' or disagreements, summarize the review and, with the participants, produce a statement of lessons learned etc.

Feedback from the trainer's observations alone

This feedback can be restricted, particularly where a number of pairs are operating at the same time. The observer can only be present at one interview at any one time, whether this is the same interview for the whole period or if the observer spends a period of time with each pair. In the latter case the observer has no grounds on which to give realistic feedback because of the limited observation. The former will suffer from the aspects mentioned earlier, in that the trainer is one person, with one person's views, which, because they come from the trainer and not the fellow course members, may not be completely accepted. However, they may be accepted if the group believes that the trainer has expertise and skill in observation and feedback, and therefore has something relevant to offer.

Feedback by both trainer and peers

If the feedback is principally given by the course member observers the trainer can play a useful role in:

- drawing attention to important points omitted from the feedback
- making some personal comments (care should be taken here)
- summarizing the learning points that have emerged from the feedback.

Feedback using CCTV observation

If the interaction has been observed and recorded with CCTV equipment feedback can take place in a number of ways. Note that the use of CCTV almost always involves an increase in the time required for feedback. Methods include:

1. Live observation by watching the interaction on the CCTV monitor immediately followed by feedback.
2. Self-feedback by the participant(s) immediately after the interaction.
3. Self-feedback, with trainer support, at the end of the formal training day.

Feedback with CCTV support

Method (1) can add considerably to the time required for feedback and can be managed in two ways:

1. Verbal feedback by the observers based on the video observation.
2. Verbal feedback supported whenever necessary by playback of the CCTV recording.

The first verbal feedback is the same as direct, live observation feedback, the paramount benefit being during the observation period when a live observer is not present to intrude. Otherwise, the two methods are the same.

In the second case the feedback procedure as described for live peer observers is followed, the main difference being that reference can be made to the video recording to emphasize a feedback point, or if the participants query the feedback. During the interaction the observers will, in addition to making notes about specific incidents, have noted the digital counter on the video recorder. This can be used to find the recorded incident, otherwise a lot of time can be wasted searching for it.

An alternative to the general feedback, CCTV feedback support can focus on the observers noting specific incidents giving feedback on these incidents alone.

Self-feedback using CCTV recordings

In addition to supporting direct, verbal feedback, CCTV recordings can be used more or less on their own to offer self-feedback to participants, particularly the principal participant in an interview role play.

The CCTV recording can be used by:

- The participant(s) not taking part in the next section of the training event but, in a separate room, viewing the recording and drawing any lessons from it. A session can be included later in the day for the participants to raise questions about their recordings, or they can refer to the trainer at the end of the formal training day.
- The participant(s) can view the recording in the evening following the training day, when the trainer can be available to assist with any problems or queries that might arise.
- The participant(s) can take a copy of the video recording away with them when they leave the training event, so that they can study the recording at home or at work, in the latter case perhaps with their manager present.

THE ESSENTIAL APPROACH TO ROLE PLAYS

It will be recognized that approaches to role playing, as indeed to any people skills event, are basically simple, requiring an open approach. Full observation and appraisal through feedback of what is happening or has happened is essential and, although the trainer has a critical part to play, the learning is built on or destroyed by the participants. First, they must participate in the role plays fully, openly and honestly to make them as realistic as possible. The participants must practise appropriate behaviour, both when participating and when giving feedback, and in the words they use to describe events (words that in some cases may include traumatic, disturbing and even hurtful comments), while also demonstrating caring, enlightening, supportive and helpful views.

Because of the very personal nature of this particular people skills training, reactions will be different from those of the more traditional approach to training or to technical and/or procedural training. Each new day of a course can herald completely different people reactions, but if the event has been successful the participants will have grown in skill, awareness, openness, behaviour and people competence, ready to have real-life interactions back at work.

11

Some Group Approaches to People Skills

This chapter:

- describes and discusses sensitivity training approaches in the form of T-Groups and encounter groups
- describes Transactional Analysis and NLP and their use in training and development in people skills.

Training and development in people skills takes place in events in which the training group is divided (particularly for practical work) into pairs or trios – it is here that we find most of the role play situations described in Chapter 10. But a number of specific training approaches are built around group development, although within the group there is substantial individual development. These latter approaches include:

> Interpersonal development
>   – Unstructured and structured
> Team development
> Other specific skills such as
>   – Negotiation
>   – Assertiveness
>   – Influencing, etc

The specific skills are text and training subjects in themselves and full descriptions, advice and guidance will be found elsewhere. This is because, although they are people skills, they require additionally training and development in particular techniques.

Other than these specific people skills, most people training in groups falls into the interpersonal or interactive skills categories, and a number of approaches have been developed to try to develop these skills. The approaches generally achieve most when the learners participate in groups so that the maximum variety of people approaches can be seen and the individuals can obtain feedback from a number of people. Much of this training is concerned with people's behaviour – what it is, what causes it, what effects it has on others, whether it needs modifying, whether it can be modified and so on.

Interpersonal skills training is not easy. Specific skills training usually has a firm base in recognized techniques or procedures and the behaviour is an add-on to these. The bases for interpersonal skills training are the many models of human behaviour that exist, principally from the disciplines of psychology and psychiatry and their therapeutic applications. Training events are consequently run according to the philosophy and personal approach of the particular trainer or organization, and each can argue strongly for their own particular approach, albeit with mainly subjective arguments.

Many people have the impression that human behaviour is part of someone's personality, and a fixed and immovable part at that. The many interpersonal skills programmes counteract this view, and demonstrate that an individual's behaviour can be modified to make that individual's approach to people situations more appropriate and therefore stand a greater chance of success.

PERSONALITY v BEHAVIOUR

Behaviour is part of an individual's activities and actions and can be quite different from their inherent personality. Behaviour can be modified, but it is rare that personality can be changed, certainly not by what we understand as training and development. Many traits that are seen and accepted as inherent personality factors are often wrongly identified and consequently are accepted as immovable. But many are simply behavioural aspects, often learned behaviour, that can be modified if the individual is made aware of:

- the effect of their behaviour on others
- the reflection of the behaviour on themselves in the eyes of others
- the existence of other behaviours that may be more appropriate.

We have to be careful how we describe the behaviour of people: 'good' and 'bad', 'best' and 'worst' are ineffective, as behavioural achievement depends on the situation in which it occurs or is used. Consequently more realistic terms are 'appropriate' and 'inappropriate' behaviours. Every situation can demand a different approach, however minor, although some situations have relatively consistent requirements.

For example, it will be rare for the chairperson of a meeting to deviate from the recognized summarizing behaviour from one meeting to another; most problem-solving meetings will follow consistent behavioural aspects of seeking ideas, proposing, seeking clarification etc. Training events involving people skills must recognize these consistencies and variations and develop the learning events to take account of them.

OPENNESS

Another integral part of people skills development can be demonstrated and modified and its effects assessed in group events. This can be a difficult area for people, and relates to their openness between each other and within organizations, particularly in a learning situation, in the giving and receiving of feedback. The basic premise in almost all approaches to appropriate people skills is that the more open you are with others, the more open they will be with you, and consequently interrelationships will be more effective. Conversely 'play your cards close to your chest' and so will they, with the result that relationships are less likely to be advanced. This is not to say that openness should be universally and totally applied. There are certainly occasions when it would be appropriate to limit the amount of openness, where disclosure of information, feelings, views or opinions might damage a relationship. But care has to be taken that non-disclosure is for the 'right' reasons and not just to avoid an openness that, although difficult, would improve a situation.

Many organizations themselves inhibit certain levels of openness between employees, between the organization and the employees and vice versa. Training programmes must take this into account, since to encourage openness in people from a particular organization would place them in employment danger if the organization had a very closed attitude.

PLANNING BEHAVIOUR

Although they may not disagree with the concepts of appropriate behaviour, many people follow such philosophies as 'it's best to be natural and be yourself', 'I prefer to play it off the cuff' and 'take it as it comes and react accordingly'. Although some people have an innate ability to interact like this, the majority would soon find themselves in difficulties dealing with people. Most situations, including people events, benefit from pre-planning and planned actions. Of course, an event such as preparing for a presentation (usually) allows a substantial amount of time to plan and prepare.

People interactions are much more immediate, but still afford an opportunity, albeit minimal, to consider the aspects of the interaction and the most appropriate behaviours. Exceptions to this are when the interaction has been set up beforehand, and the interactors are well advised to consider in advance such aspects as:

- how difficult the interaction will be
- what type of reaction might be expected from the other person
- how willing they may be to change their attitudes following the presentation of your views
- what particular types of behaviour you might use to achieve your objectives
- how much you know about the other person that will help you decide the above.

Many people taking part in an interaction, such as a meeting or a discussion, frequently feel frustrated because they are prevented from getting down to business straight away. Some delay or fencing around in the very early stages can be most helpful, however, as this gives all parties the opportunity to assess the temperature of the event and the various aspects of the other participants, about which they may have previously been unsure. It is difficult to assess the correct amount of time – too long and people become frustrated; too short and some may not be ready to discuss the subject openly.

WHAT ABOUT ME?

One of the many failings people frequently exhibit is the attitude of 'I'm always right'. An early and significant part of any people training event must be to modify this attitude to 'I am not always right'. As far as interpersonal skills trainers are concerned they must, as far as possible, be like Caesar's wife, and take every opportunity to ensure that their own behaviours are as appropriate as possible. Even more than many others, this is one behaviour in which change must be self-generated from a 'gotcha' realization. In people skills practice is the key element, and every opportunity must be taken to practise modification and seek feedback about how successful you are in this and how others see you. If interpersonal skills had a generic motto it could be 'Wad some Pow'r the giftie gie us, tae see oursels as ithers see us', since self-awareness is at least the first step to achieving appropriate behaviour.

UNSTRUCTURED EVENTS

T-Groups

Interpersonal or interactive people skills in training and development started to emerge in the late 1930s and 1940s and, developing from therapeutic psychology, almost certainly came from the unstructured approaches of that discipline.

T-Groups were among the earliest training events in people skills training and derived from the 'Training Group', an approach developed from the small group discussions of Kurt Lewin in the 1940s, further developed at the National Training Laboratories in the USA. A number of variations have emerged from these basic beginnings and the approaches are also known as laboratory training, encounter groups and sensitivity training, most of which are variations of the T-Group.

The philosophy of the T-Group espouses that:

- real learning comes from experiencing real situations, even though these may be in a training environment
- the situations are principally 'here and now' events rather than constructed activities
- learning will only be achieved by honest feedback within the group
- the most important part of the event is the 'here and now' happenings within the group, particularly when concerned with feelings rather than facts.

In order to achieve these philosophies, the T-Groups have objectives that include increasing:

- the sensitivity and awareness of the participants to their own feelings and reactions and those of others
- the ability of the learners to assess and analyse what is happening within the group and between individuals

- the participants' skills in adopting new behaviours and adapting existing behaviours to achieve an appropriate behavioural pattern; in giving and receiving feedback with sensitivity; in controlling and using feelings.

During a T-Group event the participants operate in an atmosphere of dual roles – the one in which they are observers of the behaviours of others and what is happening in the event, and the other in which they try to observe and assess their own behaviours and effects on others. The atmosphere also encourages them to raise issues that may arise either within themselves or within the group – pleasure, concern, anger, sorrow etc – issues that are predominantly avoided in most other forms of training (except assertiveness events) and have these explored fully within the group.

The 'trainer' has a completely different role in a T-Group to almost any other event. The fundamental role is an unobtrusive, background facilitator, adviser, guider, and resource provider. Encouragement and motivation are similarly unobtrusive roles, and the trainer must be prepared to accede to the wishes of the group if they are expressed directly – to give information, opinions or feedback – but only if requested. Input sessions are rarely presented, and usually only if requested by the group, and the trainer is not there to impose his or her views on the group in any way. Even intervention is at a minimum, the policy being to allow the group to work itself out of any holes it may have dug for itself – intervention might be a very last resort if it is obvious that the process is on the point of total collapse. This itself should be part of the learning process, as it will be concerned with helping the group to determine where and why it has gone wrong and encouraging them to do something about it, rather than telling them what they should do.

Perhaps the ultimate test of a successful T-Group trainer is whether they can leave the training room for ten minutes or more and not be missed.

T-Group processes

Although there are many variations in T-Group processes, the typical event is when a group of, say, 12 people come together in a residential centre for about two weeks, either as a 'stranger', 'cousin' or 'family' group. The course can start in a more or less traditional manner, in which the trainer introduces the event, explains his or her role, indicates the value of self- and group awareness and feedback, and that the process will be principally in the participants' own hands.

An alternative, rather more extreme beginning is when the group convenes at the advised time, day and room, but without the presence of a trainer. The group is left to start the process themselves, and the trainer does not appear for the introductions until much later. This process can be tense and uncomfortable until the group realizes that progress is in their own hands, and from that point activity, feedback and awareness start to flow naturally, the facilitator providing any resources requested. The group can even be left to decide when it feels it has learned everything it wanted to and/or needed to learn, with or without the resultant appearance of the trainer to tie up any loose ends.

T-Groups can be traumatic and even hurtful, but part of the learning is coping with these problems. Some people feel that trainer interventions should be more than the absolute minimum, particularly to avoid personal hurt, but in many groups, although the event is regarded as unstructured, this is not necessarily completely true. Certainly the course is not filled with structured exercises, activities being mainly here-and-now developments, but there can be a covert structure which can be identified by the trainer's interventions.

Encounter groups

These can be almost replicas of the T-Group, but commonly are directed almost completely at the feelings level, and the participants can be encouraged towards this with experiential activities from which they can identify a range of feelings and emotions. Typically these activities take the form of trust exercises, internally revealing activities along gestalt principles; rejection games; opinion discussions and so on. Frequently the facilitator is quite active, suggesting relevant activities and guiding and advising in the subsequent reviews and feedback sessions.

VALUE AND DANGERS OF SENSITIVITY TRAINING

A number of investigations over the years have been conducted to assess the value and dangers of sensitivity training. One major survey was conducted in 1979 and the findings can be summarized thus (the figures are very rough):

■ between 5% and 10% as being a potentially negative experience
■ their fellows saw 11% as having been hurt during the experience

- 2% were found to have sustained negative effects after seven months
- 67% of the individuals named as having been hurt were also named as having been helped
- 59% of those cited as having been hurt showed significant improvement after seven months
- in the short term, for a small number of participants, some kind of emotional reaction may be a necessary precondition to long-term change
- the groups investigated as a whole obtained positive benefits by becoming emotionally more stable and trusting and adaptable in the long term
- the relationship of the greater likelihood of adverse experience to high-risk participants – the taciturn and serious, shy and timid, introverted and self-sufficient
- risks were increased when the trainer involved was aggressive, but decreased when uninhibited and spontaneous, lively, sensitive and open
- risks increased when the training was less structured, very intimate, person centred and focused overly on the here and now.

Positive outcomes tended to occur when the conditions included:

- a learner – self-sufficient, conservative, apprehensive, somewhat tense and somewhat controlled
- the training – high degree of structure, low intimacy, little confrontation, more remote interactions, little emphasis on the here and now
- the facilitator – supportive, low level of anxiety, relaxed, low involvement, available freely.

These somewhat contradictory statements suggest overall that valuable learning can be achieved in sensitivity training, careful attention being paid to the nature of the people attending, the amount of structure, and the skill of the facilitator in handling critical, personal events.

STRUCTURED INTERPERSONAL EVENTS

Structured interpersonal events have the same aims and objectives as the unstructured, sensitivity approaches, and aim for the increase in the learners of their awareness of behaviours and their abilities to modify these to be appropriate. The principal differences, as suggested by the title, are a more structured (although not directive) approach within the event. Views, feelings, opinions and behaviour are highlighted by a series of structured activities, guided by the facilitator both in the decisions about *which* activities and in the review and feedback sessions. The use of Behaviour Analysis is common in events of this nature, and although there is always some danger of trauma and hurt in any event concentrating on feelings and behaviour, the structured approach lessens these dangers.

TRANSACTIONAL ANALYSIS

Transactional Analysis (TA) is a behavioural model that forms a basis for the understanding of and communication between people and is a frequently used approach in considering people skills in training and development.

TA had its origins in the therapy practice of Dr Eric Berne in the United States when he observed that clusters of behaviour could be identified in his patients. He evolved the concept of three basic patterns of behaviour controlled by an inner force, the ego, hence the ego states of TA.

The three ego states can be identified in a person's behaviour and so offer a means of analysing behaviour and identifying the driving forces behind this. Consequently TA extends behaviour analyses that consider overt behaviour only, to covert behavioural aspects and, indeed, personality. Berne considered that much of our personality is learned and that our behaviour reflects the experiences we have had in life and recorded on three internal 'tape recorders'. These recording are played back throughout the remainder of our lives and become our personality behaviour.

Ego stages

The three tape recordings or ego states are referred to as:

> the Parent state
> the Adult state
> the Child state

The Parent state contains all the emotions, feelings, attitudes and behaviours learned as an infant from birth to about age five, from parents or other strong parent figures. These attitudes, stances and behaviours are indelibly stamped on our perceptions at that time and are retained for playing back once we ourselves are grown up. When we act, think, behave, say things, feels as our parents used to do, our Parent state is in the act of replaying – eg 'Good boys don't do that'.

The Parent can be Critical or Nurturing, and typical words used in this state include:

Do	Don't	Should
Shouldn't	Must	Ought to
Have to	Can't	

Typical statements made by someone in the Parent mode are:

- 'Isn't this awful, the way prices seem to be going up all the time.'
- 'Yes, I'm sure it's all the fault of these new ways they have of making things.'
- 'It wasn't like this when I was young. . .'
- 'I wouldn't do that if I were you. I used to do it like. . .'

The Adult ego state is not necessarily 'grown up' and can operate at any age, being based on the learning we develop as we mature. The Adult collects information and facts before making decisions from these in a logical manner. External data is collected from what is going on around the individual and internal data from the feelings expressed by the Child and Parent states. As a result, typical Adult behaviours are:

Sensible and controlled
Reasonable and reasoned
Logical and rational
Decision based on options available
Probability considered

Verbal contributions made in the Adult state would include:

- 'What information do we have on this subject?'
- 'The latest computer data show. . ., so I suggest that. . .'
- 'Right. If we proceed. . ., the likely result will be. . . Is that the best approach or is there any other way?'

The Child state is the third tape that produces the child behaviour that is recorded during infancy, again up to about the age of five. When we were children we behaved in ways that can be identified as behaviour when we grow up. As a child we expressed *uninhibited* joy, sorrow, anger, distress, distaste or behaved compliantly, politely, creatively, or we were rebellious.

In the grown-up state the Child is expressed as:

Carefree	Curious	Funloving
Adventurous	Uninhibited in behaviour or attitude	

And uses such words as:

Let's	I want	I feel great
Why don't we	Come on then	

This is the expression of the Free Child, but the Adapted Child will be:

Overcompliant	Defiant	Rebellious
Complaining	Whining	Downcast eyes

with typical words:

Please can I	I'll try hard	Please
Thank you	Sorry	
(all at appropriate times)		

Transactions

Transactions are the TA equivalent of interactions and can operate at a variety of ego state levels. The three ego states are usually represented diagramatically as:

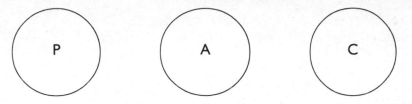

The transactions are described as:

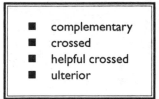

- complementary
- crossed
- helpful crossed
- ulterior

Complementary transactions

Complementary transactions take the form of interactions between people when the responses from the other person are the ones desired and expected by the initiator of the interaction. These transactions can operate at any level – Parent-Parent, Adult-Adult or Child-Child – and are acceptable events satisfying both contributors. Figure 11.1 demonstrates an Adult-Adult complementary transaction.

Figure 11.1 also shows (dotted lines) that a complementary transaction can take place between different ego states while still retaining harmony, as long as the transactional lines do not cross.

Crossed transactions

However, not all transactions are harmonious, and Crossed transactions occur when the response received is not the desired or expected response. If the initial contribution, the Child's cry for help to the Parent, does not receive a complementary response, problems will arise. Figure 11.2 demonstrates this Crossed transaction.

In this case the Child wanted the Parent to say 'Bring it here and I'll sort it out for you', but this did not happen, the Child being told to take a logical action, and this would not be well received!

Helpful crossed transactions

In general crossed transactions show that the interaction is not a harmonious one and the responses are not the ones the individuals seek. In Figure 11.3 the 'Child' appealed to the 'Parent' to do the work for them, but the 'Parent' crossed the transaction and tried to bring

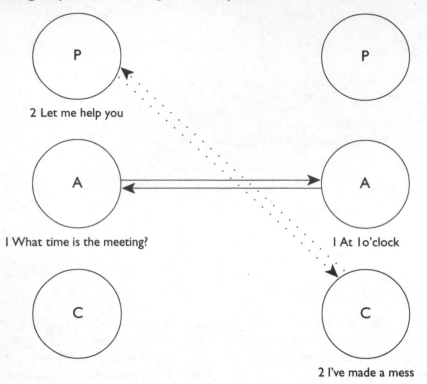

Figure 11.1 *Complementary transaction at 1. Adult level and at 2. Parent-Child, uncrossed level (dotted lines)*

the 'Child' to the 'Adult' level of transaction. This did not work on the first attempt but eventually the 'Child' moved to the 'Adult' level and started thinking about the problem in a rational way.

Ulterior transactions

Not every transaction is as obvious or overt as these examples, with psychological ones frequently taking place during what appears to be a harmonious, complementary transaction. Figure 11.4 describes such a transaction. The solid transaction lines from Adult to Adult suggest a straightforward complementary transaction, but below the surface an interaction is taking place really at the Child level. These transactions are very difficult to observe and identify, one or even both the participants not realizing what is occurring! The dotted transaction lines indicate the ulterior part of the transaction.

People training and development utilizing Transactional Analysis involves enabling the participants to become more aware of their own levels of transaction and those of others and to use this information to

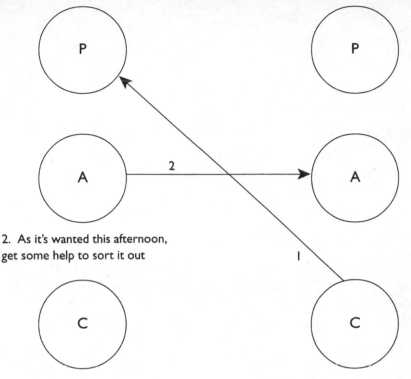

2. As it's wanted this afternoon,
get some help to sort it out

1. I've made a mess of this report

Figure 11.2 *A crosssed transaction*

achieve the desired results (naturally on an Adult-Adult level!). Activities can be included in the training with observation and self-observation to help this increasing awareness and development of effective behaviours. Simulations with briefed role play can ensure that the different roles are practised along the correct lines.

Transactional awareness

The importance of TA in people interactions is awareness of the state in which all parties are behaving and whether these are appropriate aspects of effective behaviour. Figures 11.1–11.4 have shown the initial stages of some of these possible interactions, but interactions rarely stop at this initial phase, and the skills in dealing with people involves the continuance of an effective behavioural level. Complementary transactions, if they continue at this level, present few problems and proceed satisfactorily at the agreed level to the end of the transaction, or until there is mutual agreement to change the ego state level, say

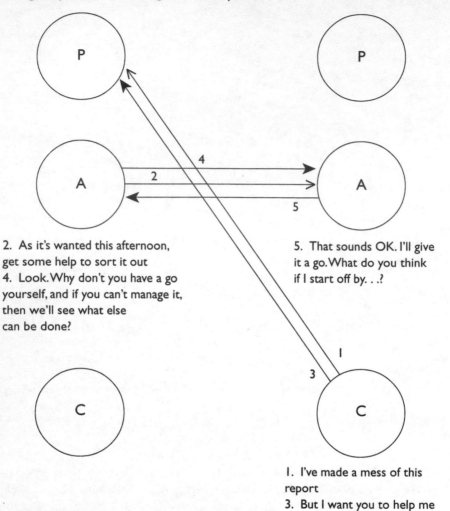

2. As it's wanted this afternoon, get some help to sort it out
4. Look. Why don't you have a go yourself, and if you can't manage it, then we'll see what else can be done?

5. That sounds OK. I'll give it a go. What do you think if I start off by. . .?

1. I've made a mess of this report
3. But I want you to help me

Figure 11.3 *A helpful crossed transaction*

from Child-Child to Adult-Adult, or Adult-Adult to Child-Child, always maintaining the complementary nature of the interaction.

The interaction described in Figure 11.3 suggested that the initial crossed Child to Parent followed by an attempt at Adult to Adult resulted eventually in an Adult-Adult transaction. However, this would not have been the only possible course of action. In the change described, the initiator may have seen that the 'Child' was open to change and consequently persevered at this approach; but the other person might be so locked into the Child state that attempts to change them to the Adult state would not only prove abortive, but could destroy the interaction.

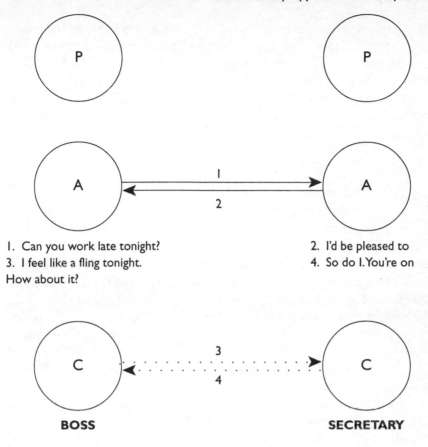

1. Can you work late tonight?
3. I feel like a fling tonight.
How about it?

2. I'd be pleased to
4. So do I. You're on

BOSS   **SECRETARY**

Figure 11.4 *An ulterior transaction*

One possible approach, which many have experienced when a heavy parental approach is used on a rebellious child (the result not always being acceptance by the child), is to switch to a grown-up Parent-Child approach demanding compliance. This may, on the surface, achieve the desired result, but may result in an ulterior attitude, residual feeling in the other person which bodes ill for future dealings.

Another option, demanding self-discipline and the use of an extended period of time that may not be available, may offer the best chance of success. If the initiator recognizes the rebellious Child state, the response may be as Parent-Child – a complementary transaction – but on this occasion not as the Critical Parent, but as the Nurturing Parent, perhaps acknowledging that 'Yes, you do seem to have got into a mess, but I know how busy you've been'. This will almost certainly result in a further Child response and the discussion might be continued at this level. Eventually the 'Child' will settle down and this may be the appropriate time to try to switch the transaction to an Adult-Adult level.

These uses of the different states, none of which is 'good' or 'bad', suggest that balanced behaviour requires awareness of the states and their effective use. Effective behaviours involve the use of all states at different times – the permanent Adult can be a bore, particularly when others want to indulge their Child states for a while, perhaps as stress release. The balanced Adult will recognize these needs and be able to switch states.

Games

Games are an important part of TA and demonstrate an additional aspect of people behaviour that must be recognized in the development of people skills. Most games are not played for positive results and many occur in the Child state. Many varieties exist, but the outcome is usually predictable. This appeals to many people as they feel it gives them a sense of security and frequently enables them to lay blame on others. Other reasons for playing games can be to receive 'strokes' or as a way of structuring time to avoid boredom – is this Adult or Child behaviour?

A typical life game is NIGYSOB (Now I've got you, you son of a bitch). It often occurs in meetings when one participant puts another down, frustrates them or denigrates them in some way. This action makes them decide to get their own back at the next opportunity, for example at the next meeting, to the exclusion of the real objectives of the meeting. Consequently all the person's efforts are directed at getting their own back; the persecuted one may realize what is happening and resist these attempts, additionally trying to score further points. As a result, two people are not being effective meeting members and are participating in effective transactional behaviour, really as Child-Child.

Rituals and pastimes

Rituals and pastimes are other people behaviours recognized by TA and can be considered safer forms of game playing, as their principal intent is more to pass the time than score points. There is always the possibility, however, that a pastime can develop into a dangerous game.

A frequent ritual in which people engage is that of the morning greeting, in which one person asks another 'How are you?' The enquirer usually has little or no interest in the actual state of health of the person greeted, the question being part of the ritual. The other person, knowing this absence of real interest, even if they are not feeling too well, will respond 'Fine, thanks', and the two pass on.

A newcomer to the ritual might break it by starting to give an account of how unwell they feel. This response is not understood by the initiator, who was expecting the ritual response, and who can be irritated by the breaking of the predictability. The other person then feels bewildered by the apparent lack of interest in the answer and future interactions can be affected.

Pastimes can take place anytime, anywhere, although they are found more frequently at social occasions or quasi-social occasions at work. Gatherings of couples are often characterized by the men grouping to take part in the pastime of discussing 'My car. . .' or 'My DIY activities. . .', while the women discuss other topics of a similar nature in another grouping.

Superficial discussions of the ritual and pastime nature are often essential in people interactions, whether at the start of an interview so that the subject is eased into it, or with a manager walking round the work area asking such questions as 'What did you think of the match last night', 'How did the holiday go', and so on. They can also be valuable when there is an exchange of members between groups, with perhaps the leader of the group taking the initiative and welcoming a new member with 'We have just been talking about X. What do you think?'

Strokes

When trying to deal with people successfully, if you are in a responsible position you should be aware of people wanting to maintain their needs for recognition, affection and attention, as identified earlier by Maslow (see Chapter 5). This is achieved by what TA refers to as 'strokes'. Children are the prime example of this need, but we tend to forget that adults have an equal, albeit often concealed need. A stroke is often awarded by the simple recognition of an achievement – 'You did a good job with that report', but care must be taken to ensure that the stroke does not sound insincere or patronizing.

People will often prefer even a negative stroke to no stroke at all – 'I wouldn't have minded if he had bawled me out for doing it; at least I would have known how he felt.' People need to know how they are doing, how others feel about them – the bouquets and the brickbats. But care must be taken not to give too many strokes, otherwise there is the danger that they may be sought for collecting's sake, and an overabundance can reduce their apparent value. Perhaps a hierarchy of strokes might be developed, with very positive, very encouraging ones retained for important instances, whereas more minor ones can be recognized by a lesser comment.

Trading stamps

People collect 'trading stamps' in addition to strokes, these in TA terms representing feelings that might be discharged at a later stage.

The trading stamps might be 'gold' ones, collected when praise, recognition or justification is given, and redeemed when the collector has a full book – that is, when they feel that sufficient good work has been recognized for them to give themselves a present. This might range from simply sitting back from work for a few minutes to taking longer periods of time off. The skilled people interactor will recognize this need and take care in confronting someone who may be in this mode.

'Brown' stamps are the opposite and are the product of bad feelings such as repressed anger, frustration, depression. Redemption of brown trading stamps is again delayed until the collector can take no more of the unjustified criticism etc – that is, when the book is full. If a non-assertive person is subdued on every occasion, eventually even the quietest mouse can take no more and if the brown book is full an 'explosion' occurs, often when the other person is not expecting this. The explosion can be violent or nothing more than throwing a piece of paper across the room or going to a colleague's room for a good grumble. But the responsible person's people skills are obviously limited because these possibilities were not assessed or identified.

TA training

The use of TA in training and development situations was mentioned briefly earlier in this chapter, and all the TA aspects – ego state analysis, transactional analysis, games, strokes, pastimes and rituals, and trading stamps – can be used as a basis for training in life and social skills and an improvement in people skills. Training is usually aimed at:

- Reducing the inappropriate outbalance of the use of Parent and Child states
- Increasing where necessary access to the Free Child
- Giving guidance in the use of positive strokes
- Increasing awareness of the use of ego states in transactions
- Increasing abilities in using ego states in transactions
- Reducing game playing or minimizing its effects
- Bringing the effects of stamp collecting into perspective
- Enabling the modification of awareness and behaviour

Training utilizing TA can range from a simple introduction to the technique, describing the elements that make up the concept, to a full training programme in life modification and enhancement of people skills. The technique can be a stand alone or part of a larger programme, usually one aimed at the development of effective behaviour and people skills.

NEURO-LINGUISTIC PROGRAMMING (NLP)

NLP has appeared only relatively recently on the training and development scene, stemming mainly from the work in the 1970s of John Grindler and Richard Bandler. It is a complex concept, principally because it is essentially an aggregation of almost all the skills required in dealing with people. If you read a description of NLP you will find that many facets have been included in many management and supervisory training and development programmes for a long period. NLP has gathered these together into a cohesive model concerned with responding effectively to other people, and understanding and respecting their views, opinions and needs – people skills. Training and development practitioners will recognize in NLP such techniques as creativity, verbal and non-verbal communication, stress management, assertiveness, modelling, influencing, and behaviour awareness and modification.

Because NLP has its roots in psychotherapy the language used can be daunting, and attitudes to the approach range from excitement and an evangelical intent to introduce it, through scepticism of its ability to transfer from therapy to training and its effectiveness as a technique, to horror and rejection. Many of its strongest proponents see it as a panacea for all training and development needs – there may be some truth in this, not because of NLP itself, but because it encompasses all the best practices for dealing effectively with people. Others, the strongest sceptics, see it as a 'flavour of the month', something that has occurred on a number of occasions in the field of training and development. But one important aspect of the NLP concept, and one with which few can disagree, is that people skills are anchored in communication, and effective communication can only be measured by the response you receive.

Some aspects of NLP

Some of the aspects of NLP that have a direct relevance to use in training and development include:

> Matching
> Mirroring
> Pacing and Leading
> Eye cues
> Calibration

Matching. As the name suggests, this is the action of matching the tone and tempo of your voice and your breathing rate to that of the person to whom you are speaking. If they speak softly, so do you; if they speed up, so do you; but always without obviously mimicking or aping or being too extreme in your matching. The model suggests that this matching will subconsciously flatter the other person, who will see and accept you as being in tune with them. This will help in the establishment of rapport.

Mirroring. This aspect on non-verbal communication has been recognized as an effective approach for a long time. It involves a deliberate mirroring of the other's posture, attitude and body language – sometimes we do this unconsciously with a positive effect. If it is done consciously, we are improving our chances of establishing the rapport that is so important in people interactions and the use of people skills.

One example of this mirroring includes sitting forward when the other person does. Usually this occurs during a period when the emotion in a discussion is rising and the person wants to ensure that their points are understood and accepted; mirroring the movement, 'tells' that person that you recognize this importance and are willing to listen and consider. Smiling is a behaviour we frequently produce when the other person smiles at us – this is probably our most unconscious form of mirroring, but again a deliberate action can have the desired effect. Many forms of mirroring – for example, folding your arms when the other does – have to be done carefully and subtly so that the other person does not get the impression that you are mocking them, but performed carefully the other person's subconscious will recognize and react to the empathic action.

This is mirroring described in positive terms, but it can also be used in a more negative manner. A 'typical' boss-subordinate attitude is for the boss to clasp his or her hands behind their head and lean back in their chair, suggesting dominance because they have nothing to fear from the subordinate. If these actions are mirrored, eventually the boss can start to think 'What's going on here. My dominance is being challenged/negated', even if they do not realize that actual mirroring is taking place.

Pacing and leading. This does not refer to pacing about physically, but recognizing and respecting the emotional state or feeling of the other person. For example, if the other person is demonstrating anger, pacing does not involve being angry in turn but demonstrating that you recognize their anger and see the reason for it. If the reason for the anger is justifiable, you can also show support and the desire to care for and help them. Again the intention of these actions is to establish a rapport that will help the interaction to proceed smoothly and effectively, in most cases the pacing changing to a leading of the other person into a more acceptable state.

Eye cues. Known in NLP as VAK (visual, auditory and kinaesthetic responses), these are, in many ways, an extension of standard non-verbal eye signals, but NLP suggests that specific eye movements will tell an observer how the other person is thinking during the communication, although, as in the case of NVC generally, other NVC clues must support the eye cues observations. One possible snag in observing these effects is that they involve looking very directly at the eyes of the other person. This can be a difficult way of communicating for many people and can involve them in embarrassing situations.

Although the eye clues are not universal in application, they suggest that right-handed people are:

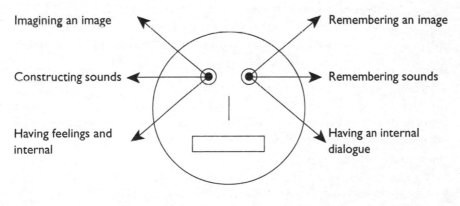

Figure 11.5 *Eye cues*

If the person is looking straight forward, but in an unfocused way, they will be either creating or remembering visual images.

So:

- a movement of the eyes upwards and to the right or left or straight ahead, means that the person's recall is visual
- movement to the side means that the person is auditorily constructing or remembering words or sounds so that they can access the information
- movement downwards means that they are recalling sounds or words, smells or tastes.

Calibration. This is claimed by NLP to be the key to effective communication and is described as the reading of other people, their eye and facial movements, breathing, and other forms of non-verbal signals. Using all the available signals you can try to assess the feelings of the other person and how effective your inter-communication is being. There are no rules by which you can be guided as every interaction will be different, just as people are different, and you will need to use all your skills of people observation to pick up the signals that will enable you to calibrate the interaction.

NLP training

A basic NLP training and development course will concentrate on a full understanding and appreciation of the concepts and ideas expressed in the model, in addition to ensuring practice in the skills. But, like TA, these concepts can be applied to more general training and development and Sally Dimmick (1995) suggests how the three representational systems – visual, auditory and kinaesthetic – can be brought together to maximize communication and learning.

The visual representation area

The visual representation area of learning will be strengthened by the extensive use of visual media:

OHPs
Flipcharts
Whiteboards
Handouts
Course notes
Videos
Photographic slides
Film strips
Computer slides

The learners' visual preferences will also be influenced by other physical effects such as:

The training room
   — Décor
   — Lighting
   — Layout
   — Decorations
The trainer
   — Appearance
   — Manner
   — Clothing

The auditory representational system

Many of the effects in this area were discussed earlier in the communication section of this book and primarily involve such aspects as:

Listening
Barriers to listening
The use of the voice
The use of words
Questioning

Other auditory aspects that will have an effect on the learning include:

Using audio tapes
Effective input sessions
Discussions

The kinaesthetic representational system

NLP, in company with most effective training and development programmes, recognizes the prime importance of active participation in learning, particularly for those with kinaesthetic preferences (the Activists and Pragmatists of the Honey/Mumford Learning Preferences). A number of factors have been recognized as having a learning effect in this area:

Activities or games
  – Icebreakers
  – Introductory exercises
  – Refreshers
  – Simulations
  – Ending exercises
Role plays
Case studies
Group activities
  – Structured
  – Unstructured
Interactive programmes
  – Video
  – Computer

In addition to specific training techniques that will appeal to those with kinaesthetic preferences other approaches, many of which have parallels in other systems, can be included:

Notetaking
Handouts
Object handling

Notetaking, in the first instance, would appear to be more relevant to visual representation, and indeed there is common usage, but one important element of the practice during a training event of whatever nature is the movement of the learner away from passivity to a greater degree of activity. In an input session, for example, if the learners simply sit and listen, learning may be at a minimum because of their passive attitude. Active notetaking decreases the passivity and should encourage a greater degree of learning. Any form of notetaking will be useful, but in the atmosphere of NLP a creative form such as patterned note-taking may be the one to encourage.

Handouts similarly are linked with visual representation, but can be used in an active manner. For example, rather than just giving the learners the handouts to read at the end of the event, they can be used *during* the event as part of the active learning process. A handout might require readers to take some action before continuing with the text – this could be used on more than one occasion. Or, during the session the learners, having been given the handout to read, are invited to initiate a discussion on the content or, particularly if a controversial aspect has been included, to come to conclusions about, say, the relevance to them of one path or another.

The design of a training and development programme, whether or not the designers subscribe to NLP, will benefit from the total concepts of NLP on the basis that learning appears to be more readily achieved if the processes are varied and are formed so as to appeal to learners with a range of representational preferences. Ted Garratt (1997) lists the uses of NLP in training programmes as being 'evident and useful in every aspect of training. From creating rapport, through to establishing outcomes, to modelling strategies for success'. He also identifies specific training programmes in which it can be used:

Any form of interviewing	Creating corporate culture
Team building	People skills
Coaching	Presentations
Mentoring	Interpersonal skills
Negotiating	Effective meetings
Selling	Leadership
Change management	Motivation
Risk management	Influencing and persuading
Outdoor training progammes	

This list encompasses a very wide range of the types of training and development used today and is notable by the fact that all the programmes included are strongly biased towards people skills.

12

—

Team Building and Development

This chapter:

■ describes effective teams and the barriers to their development and the role of the team leader
■ considers the use of the Belbin and Team Management Resource models in team role development
■ describes and advises on the four stages of team building and development, and summarizes the problems encountered in developing a team.

Teams can be considered the ultimate in people skills where a group of people is concerned. The approaches and techniques described so far have dealt with the training and development in people skills of individuals, whether in small or larger groups. Team building and development brings these people together, perhaps after they have engaged in more personal development or they develop with the team. Team development appears to be most effective when the team itself, including its leader, meets in the building and development of activities and events. If there is a more separate approach it is essential that, before the team process can be considered complete and effective, the team takes part in composite team training events.

AN EFFECTIVE TEAM

A number of criteria can be used to identify an effectively functioning team, towards which goal a developing team should be aiming:

■ the team has clear objectives
■ the people care for each other

- the team members are open with each other
- there is a high level of trust
- decisions are made within the team by consensus or a fully agreed alternative
- people are committed to the team and its development
- conflict is faced and resolved within the team
- people listen not only to ideas, information and opinions, but also to feelings that can be expressed freely
- team roles can be identified and members identify with them
- the team works as effectively as possible to achieve the team tasks
- there are sound relationships with other groups or teams.

From this it will be obvious that a group of people working together in a work unit do not necessarily make a team. Without the above degrees of interactivity and interdependence focused on an agreed goal, objective or task, and the process by which it will be achieved, the group is simply a group of people. Synergy best describes the difference between groups and teams, in that in a group 5 + 5 = 10 (hopefully) whereas in a team the synergic sum would be 5 + 5 = 11 (or even more).

TYPES OF TEAMS

Even with satisfaction of the criteria listed above, a team can be identified further by using three dimensions of team activity.

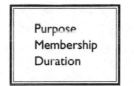

Purpose
Membership
Duration

Purpose

Every team must have a purpose, an objective or aim; this may have been imposed, but preferably should have been agreed by the team. This purpose will almost invariably be task oriented – product development and operation, quality control, system management etc.

Membership

Like the purpose, the membership of the team may be imposed, but obviously this could make the team's development more difficult, even on occasions impossible. The membership should be role comprehensive, whether drawn from a single discipline or multi-disciplines, each member having a specific purpose. The hierarchical level of the team can vary, from a team consisting of the top, senior management; through a work unit team with a line manager; to a work unit team led by a supervisor within a unit containing several teams.

Duration

The team might be a permanent feature or a temporary one formed to satisfy a specific aim or task. The latter, particularly if its life is to be relatively short, can be a difficult team to build, develop and lead, and may never achieve real team status because of a lack of motivation stemming from its temporary nature.

BARRIERS TO EFFECTIVE TEAM DEVELOPMENT

Nothing ever runs completely smoothly, and teams are no exception. If a non-team or non-effective team is examined, it might be seen to exhibit some or all of the following barriers. None of these is insurmountable given the will to develop the team, although it must be admitted that power distribution can sometimes make their modification more difficult.

1. Over-control by the leader
2. Inappropriate leadership style
3. Power conflicts among the members
4. Lack of support from fellow team members
5. Restriction of creative attitudes and attempts
6. Isolation, or imagined isolation by individuals
7. Poor, or no definition of an individual's role in the team
8. Poorly defined aims and objectives for the team and its tasks
9. Overemphasis on procedures and details
10. Too quick a response without due consideration
11. Firefighting rather than planned action

12. Uncertainty about levels of personal and corporate authority and responsibility
13. Difficult communication
14. Lack of understanding among members and limited respect for each other
15. Unresolved differing values
16. A non-supportive corporate culture
17. Personal limitations
18. Limited team skills
19. Wrong mix of skills
20. Numerical outbalance.

From the above list it is obvious that the formation of an effective team that can overcome the barriers is not a simple task. Many forces push against effectiveness, and a substantial amount of hard work is necessary to produce a better balance. Some of these barriers require further consideration and clarification.

THE TEAM LEADER

It may appear a pedantic play on words, but a team needs a leader rather than a manager. The simple difference here is that the manager is in a more controlling position, giving instructions and telling, whereas the leader is very much an integral part of the team, facilitating the team and task processes, and being very concerned with the needs of the team as individuals and as a whole. In many effective teams it is often difficult to identify the leader or senior person, the apparent and practical leadership moving from one member to another as varying needs arise.

The role of the team leader can be defined in four principal areas:

Contracting
Communicating
Facilitating
Evaluating

Contracting

This is a particularly relevant function when a new team is being created or an existing team is being required to take on new or modified tasks. Aspects of this function will include:

- representing the team with more senior management and receiving task instructions
- briefing the team on new or modified tasks
- ensuring understanding of the tasks
- leading discussion on the task, its aims and objectives, and reaching team agreement on these
- discussing and agreeing terminal standards for the task
- agreeing the allocation of roles and tasks among the team members.

Communicating

- keeping the team informed of all relevant information – task progress, changed requirements, contacts with other teams or work units etc.
- receiving, collating and disseminating to the other members of the team ideas that have been proposed by individuals or sub-groups, information and task progress where this impinges on the roles of others
- calling and/or agreeing to meetings and task review sessions
- identifying problems arising and taking relevant problem-solving action (not necessarily solving the problem, but using a team problem-solving event)
- responsibility for communicating with sponsors or other senior management, and with other teams or groups, except when this has been delegated to a team member.

Facilitating

- monitoring and reviewing the progress of the task and initiating or requiring any action to resolve difficulties
- taking personal interest in team members, supporting, motivating, encouraging and disciplining as necessary
- reviewing progress of the work towards task achievement and taking relevant action
- calling problem-solving meetings as necessary and guiding the team in the decision-making process

- identifying and/or agreeing individual and team training and development needs and taking the necessary supportive action
- performing his or her own task role.

Evaluating

- reviewing, with individuals or the team, progress and achievements towards the agreed task objectives
- reviewing with the team its progress in the team development process and offering feedback.

PERSONAL AND TEAM LIMITATIONS

The strength of any team and the factors ensuring the desired synergy is determined by the strength of its weakest link, whether this is an individual or the team process itself. If the team is an established one, with well-defined tasks of a relatively permanent nature, the approach to ensuring the necessary skills should be fairly simple. The role of each member will be defined and the basic requirement that they have the necessary skills to perform their role fulfilled.

The identification of training and development skill needs when new tasks have to be performed by the team should be equally simple. It may be that the team members have the skills required, or at least some of them. An effectively working team will be able to identify as a team where these skills lie and where there are shortfalls. Training and development can then be arranged.

The more difficult area usually found in team development is the working of the team itself, rather than the individuals. The aspects of an effective team have been described earlier: some of these can be relatively easily developed within the team as it follows its normal operation, others may need special team training. Unfortunately many of the team skills are divorced from the task skill requirements, being the special team unification skills that ensure a cohesive group of people. Any failings here can frequently only be remedied over a long period of time within the team, avoiding as many as possible of the barriers listed earlier. Some skills might be improved by training event attendance – for example, interpersonal skill awareness where feedback by 'strangers' may be more impactive than if given by people who are very close. Often a more effective approach is to coach, mentor or train internally, a team event being used for the purpose, such as team 'teach-ins' on creative thinking and brainstorming, using real problems in these events. The team development skills of the training department may be useful in supporting or facilitating in these cases.

Numerical outbalance

A team will find it difficult to operate effectively if its numbers are wrong or out of balance. This effect can be produced by too many or too few members. If there are too many:

- there may be insufficient tasks or roles for all members to participate fully and without jealousy
- insufficient involvement reduces commitment and motivation
- sub-groups or cliques can develop introducing conflict or undesirable competition within the team
- team roles start to overlap and become unclear; as a result team members themselves become unclear about their places in the team
- the team leader will find it problematical to maintain a finger on the pulse of the team, to maintain an integrated role in the team, to know the individuals to a desirable extent; and may need to become more 'managerial'.

If there are too few members:

- too many roles and tasks will be imposed on the individuals and the work rate can suffer
- an outbalance of task distribution because of skill variations can occur
- some team roles may not be filled
- wider aspects of creativity may be missing as a result of reduced input of ideas and cross-fertilization
- the team leader may be encouraged to take on too many personal tasks and start to fail in the proper role.

The most effective number will depend on a variety of circumstances. Some tasks will require many individuals, other tasks fewer. But whatever the task or the size of the task, an effective team requires at least one member able to fulfil each of the team roles (these are considered later). A useful rule-of-thumb with which most team leaders agree is a number between six and ten – more than this, unless the group is subdivided into several teams, the group becomes too unwieldy to operate as a team.

A NON-SUPPORTIVE CORPORATE CULTURE

If for any reason – frequently fear of employee strength – the organization does not encourage, or even discourages, the formation of real teams, team development can be a long path, if the end is ever reached. Development should be approached slowly and deliberately, one step at a time, effective results speaking to the organization to encourage its support.

Frequently lack of support stems from lower in the organization than the corporate whole. Many managers fail to develop teams, however much proof can be offered of their value. Two principal fears can be the cause of this. The manager realizes that the traditional management role and power is changed within the team concept, is afraid of this and wants to retain power and/or control. Or, the manager has an incomplete understanding of team benefits and development and is afraid to try to introduce teamworking in case it fails and a loss of face results.

The training and development department can help by a process of education. In the first case the manager realizes that his or her role becomes even more important with teamworking, and in the second case the manager is given team leading skills, so reducing any fear.

MEMBERSHIP PROBLEMS

One of the principal barriers to the development of an effective team is a lack of understanding among the team members of each other's needs, values, feelings and attitudes. Without this understanding there will be distance between the members that inhibits the necessary team relationship. On many occasions this relationship develops naturally as the team grows, but sometimes, particularly in the case of new teams, special measures are necessary. These can usefully be introduced by a series of team training events, following a pattern of interpersonal skills and sensitivity training described in Chapter 11. The team can take part in a series of activities that introduce increasingly more personal exercises so that the team members can develop a greater understanding of each other's skills, behaviours and attitudes. Programmes of this nature frequently end with a process in which the participants contract with each other to exhibit or not exhibit certain behaviours. This is often a horse-trading exercise in which written agreements are exchanged between the members, stating 'I will do (or not do, or continue to do) so-and-so, if you do (or not do or continue to do) so-and-so'. A feature of succeeding team process meetings can be discussion on the achievement, or otherwise, of the agreements. The intention is that the events on the programme and the resulting agreements will increase mutual awareness, understanding, trust and openness, essential elements of the effective team.

TEAM ROLES

A number of models enable consideration of essential team roles that, in addition to task skills and performance, support the effective team. The models express the ideal, a particularly problematical situation if an existing team is inherited or team members are allocated without any reference to team needs. Two major models are current, one by R M Belbin (1981), the other developed by C J Margerison and D J McCann (1984).

The Belbin model

The basis of Belbin's model is the identification of nine essential team roles that he labels:

Co-ordinator
Shaper
Plant
Monitor-evaluator
Resource investigator
Implementer
Team worker
Completer
Specialist

A team should include people who can carry out these roles, although this does not necessarily mean that one person relates to one role only – some members of the team may be efficient at more than one. Problems may arise if the team includes two or more who have the same role profiles but who may not have compatible ideas and attitudes. This will be particularly the case with the Shaper or Resource Investigator, less so with the Team Worker or Monitor-Evaluator, although even here compatibility is essential.

It must be stressed that within the profiles there is no best or worst role and members will sometimes have two or even more role preferences. Team members rarely consider themselves in these roles without discussion, most people doing things in the team almost without thinking. What should be avoided if at all possible is to have a team member behave in a role in which they do not feel comfortable – they will as a result not do a very good job.

The roles are described as follows.

Co-ordinator

- recognizes the skills of the individuals and how they can be used
- pulls people and tasks together
- has a strong sense of the team objectives and can clarify these
- tries to maintain harmony among the team members
- good at controlling people and events and co-ordinating resources, although may not be the leader.

Shaper

- a natural leader who can command respect and motivate and enthuse others, provided the negative behaviours are controlled
- an outgoing and dominant person who has to be careful not to be domineering
- urges the team to achievement of the team objectives
- impatient with complacency and lack of progress and can over-react
- can be provocative and insensitive to others' feelings
- likes to have own ideas accepted
- has energy and determination to overcome obstacles.

Plant

- an ideas person, full of creativity
- usually a dominant person, but can be serious minded and introverted
- can be tactless and lacking sensitivity to others in pursuit of the ideas
- dislikes orthodoxy and not too concerned with practicalities
- potentially the most creative member of a team, sometimes 'planted' in a team for this purpose.

Monitor-evaluator

- the logical, analytical, objective processor in the team
- tends to be unobtrusive until special qualities needed
- cautious and critical of loose thinking in others
- not imaginative or creative, but suggests team consider alternatives (but logically).

Resource investigator

- the 'outside contact' member, rarely in the office
- extroverted, outgoing, enthusiastic when investigating anything new
- can stimulate discussion, but soon gets tired after initial buzz
- close involvement with people
- a grasshopper
- skilled at finding and starting to use resources.

Implementer

- a stable, self-disciplined member, aware of the team's obligations internally and externally
- very practical and needs convincing of the practicality of new ideas
- conservative and reactionary
- happy when involved in working out methods, procedures, and rules for implementation.

Team worker

- works well with different people and can be depended on to promote a good team atmosphere, helping the team to gel
- diplomatic and sensitive to the feelings of others, not seen as a threat
- supportive and a good listener, able to recognize and resolve the development of conflict and other difficulties.

Completer

- an introverted perfectionist, interested in detail and seeking high standards in self and others
- relentless in following tasks through to the bitter end
- finishes tasks thoroughly, giving them complete attention
- can antagonize others through the over-attention to detail and nitpicking.

Specialist

- the member with specialist knowledge, skill and ability
- dedicated to and enthusiastic about the specialism, but tends to be remote from the team until the services are required.

Most people will recognize these role descriptions, in themselves or in others, although perhaps self-identification might not always be objective. Questionnaires and tests can be used to obtain or confirm the identification and produce a profile of the team.

The team management resource

Margerison and McCann suggested a different kind of model of team behaviour, based on eight main roles within an effective team, but directly relating the roles to key work functions. The model can be shown graphically in a circle or wheel, the team task process following round the wheel (Figure 12.1).

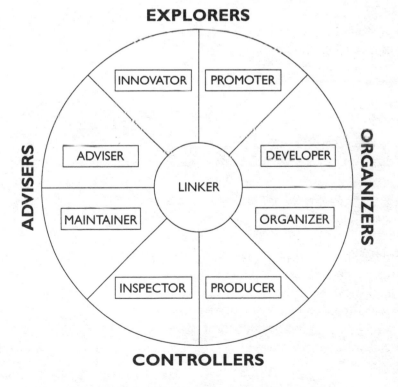

Figure 12.1 *The team management 'wheel'*

The role descriptions identified within the wheel can be applied equally to tasks and people and are as follows.

Advisers

- information gatherers
- experience users
- advisers on researched details
- supportive
- flexible
- set high standards
- knowledgeable.

Innovators

- imaginative and with vision
- intuitive and creative
- independent and information gatherers
- researchers and innovators.

Promoters

- explorers
- persuasive of others to take up ideas
- active, outgoing and easily bored
- creative and searching
- project oriented and resource contractors.

Developers

- test the applicability of new ideas
- develop new ideas into prototypes with which to experiment
- outgoing
- analytical, testing, planning.

Organizers

- make things happen through implementation
- action persons who are result oriented
- analytical, set up systems and negotiate toughly
- determined, time conscious and often impatient
- organize people to perform the tasks.

Producers

- practical people concerned with results
- organized, systematic, deadline conscious
- have regular output following planning
- take pride in producing the goods.

Inspectors

- check and audit process to ensure installed systems are working effectively
- detail oriented, thorough, conscientious
- reflective and look to standards
- can be seen as negative and criticizers

Maintainers

- ensure that effective systems and processes continue to be operated for as long as necessary
- supporters and helpers within the team
- strong values and high standards
- reflective and conscientious, but reluctant to make changes

Linkers

- come from any of the other roles and work in a co-ordinating way
- integrate people and activities
- brokers and linkers
- good communicators
- can be several in a team.

The team role descriptions summarized above can be applied equally to people and functions. If a new task is proposed for a team, for example, the logical path to achievement would be as follows.

The cycle starts in the area of advising and includes:

1. Obtain as much information as possible about the task, precedents, other practices, research information and so on – the role and function of the Adviser.
2. Offer or produce various options for the methods, procedures, systems and practices – the Innovator.
3. Pick up the creative ideas, assess their value and sell the most appropriate ones – the Promoter.

The next role/function moves the cycle on to a more logical and pragmatic sector in which it is necessary to:

4. Assess the options and put these forward with ways and means of achieving the task – the Developer.
5. Implement the agreed option following organization of the process and people and the action pressed – the Organizer.
6. Ensure an outcome and that the processes are actually implemented – the Producer.

The final stage is entered when the task is in operation and the actions then include:

7. Ensuring that agreed systems, practices, regulations and standards are being followed accurately – the Inspector.
8. Ensuring that the wheels run smoothly over the (perhaps extended) period, during which the task continues, and that nothing is lost after the initial impetus – the Maintainer.

While this team process is taking place the various functions and roles need to be co-ordinated in different ways. These are the functions of linking and the Linker.

When another new task emerges the process restarts either at the Adviser stage or later in the cycle depending on the nature of the task. Some teams, performing particular tasks, may require all the roles, others the later roles and functions only, so the definition of the effectiveness of the team will relate to the functional needs. An ultimate, though unrealistic aim would be for every team member to fulfil every team role. But different people have different strengths and preferences and these should be used, ensuring that all necessary roles and functions are covered, preferably with duplicating reserves.

Usually people are found to have preferences for and strengths in several roles – the secondary preferences are generally found in nearby roles. For example it is common for the Innovator to have some interest in the Promoter and Adviser roles. A less likely combination would be the separated roles of the Innovator and Inspector.

THE TEAM DEVELOPMENT PROCESS

Whichever role model is followed, and neither conflicts with the other, the team leader must ensure that all required roles and functions are covered by at least one member for each role. Consequently training and development may be necessary, either to 'top up' an existing team or to develop a new team from scratch. In fact both types of teams can be considered 'new', since the existing team that lacks some aspects may not really be a 'team'.

Two aspects of the development process should be considered: (a) the overall process itself and (b) the effects of the stages of the process.

The team process

We have seen that the essence of teamwork is where the members work together towards a common goal, respecting each others' abilities and failings and, in addition, progressing towards the completion of the task, are interested and active in the team development process. Consequently a team development process involves the team's progress as a coherent whole, the achievement of the task and the development of each individual within this.

John Adair (1986) expresses this in the three circle model of Task, Team and Individual, shown in Figure 12.2.

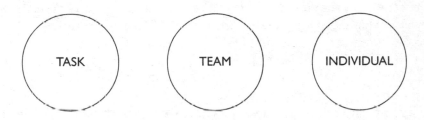

Figure 12.2 *The three circle team process*

The model identifies the team process as requiring the satisfaction of the three factors, not as discrete, independent aspects, but as overlapping, mutually dependent areas. If the needs of only the group receive attention the completion of the task can suffer and the individuals might not support the group needs but concentrate on their individual needs that might not be satisfied. This is demonstrated graphically in Figure 12.3 by the overlap of the circles, the amount of overlap depending on the variety of factors that demand attention. If the needs of the individuals and the group are treated in a balanced way, and the task requirements receive similar treatment, task achievement and people progress are much more likely.

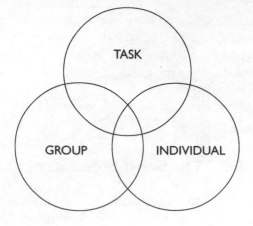

Figure 12.3 *The overlapping circles team process*

THE TEAM BUILDING PROCESS

In order to satisfy the balanced requirements suggested by Adair, we need to have a team which, as suggested earlier, may need to be developed from scratch. This apparently is a simple case of ensuring that the individuals possess all the appropriate skills and are aware of and active in behaving as a *team* rather than a group of people. This development, however, is far from simple, particularly with regard to the development of the individuals as a team.

Following a considerable amount of research by observers of groups and teams, a major conclusion has been reached about the stages that most groups and teams pass through as they develop, these stages being virtually predictable and, to some extent, controllable. The four stages are commonly described as:

> Stage 1: Forming
> Stage 2: Storming
> Stage 3: Norming
> Stage 4: Performing

Each stage is quite readily identified and in the majority of cases follows a cycle, any stage being rarely omitted, except perhaps in the case of an existing group that is trying to develop into a team. In this case, stage 1 may not occur and some aspects of stage 2 may be missing, although beware of assumptions. The stages are represented graphically in Figure 12.4.

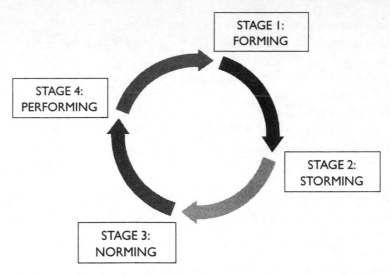

Figure 12.4 *The four stage team development process*

Forming

This stage is sometimes known by the title 'Confusion' as this can represent accurately the state of mind of the new team members coming together initially. The stage of development will be at a low, immature level, the members being in an unusual situation and reacting to this.

Typical behaviours in this stage, certainly in the early parts of it, include:

- Uncertainty
- Confusion
- Where am I?
- Closed attitude to others
- Cautious
- Reserved
- Polite
- Withholding true feelings
- Wondering about personal acceptance
- What is going to happen?
- Will I be able to cope?

This uncertain behaviour pattern will be based on a set of 'rules', rules that are either generally understood or are assumed:

- avoid disclosing too much personal information
- if discussing feelings, do so in a minimum way
- avoid serious or deep topics
- avoid movement towards the emergence of feelings
- avoid controversy
- present simple ideas
- make statements that will almost certainly be acceptable
- play it cool for a while
- if not already decided, what sort of role am I going to present?

As the group starts to settle down with the passage of time, other feelings (usually undisclosed) will emerge. These will include:

- Impatience with the lack of progress
- Impatience with an apparent absence of structure and purpose
- Feelings of wanting to be somewhere else
- Feelings of hostility to leader and other members
- Continuing not to communicate fully
- Feeling uncomfortable in the silences and pauses
- Seeking leader help and guidance

During this period of confusion, uncertainty and the membership seeking structure, purpose and guidance, the team leader (or, in a team building training event, the trainer) plays a vital part and can be significantly responsible for (a) the success of the stage and (b) the length of time in which the group stays in the stage.

Some key team building activities here include:

- being aware of, identifying and acknowledging, without denigrating them, the attitudes and feelings of the individuals
- encouraging expectations, hopes, worries and concerns to emerge openly – this might be achieved by using a 'Hopes/Concerns' T-Chart, initially concerned with the event itself, then moving on to feelings
- suggesting 'rules' for the event, discussing these with the group and obtaining as much agreement as possible
- using team building techniques, particularly active and experiential ones rather than passive listening.

The basic aspect of the 'team' in this stage is one of dependency on the 'leader' and, as development occurs, the start of a team entity, however superficial this may be. However, one attitude that may prevent progress or bode ill for development is the forming of liaisons or cliques. This is natural when the individuals start to find others who appear to have similar attitudes etc to them to whom they look for support.

Storming

The group starts moving out of the forming stage as attitudes and feelings start to emerge more strongly, and attitudes of competition, conflict and the bidding for power start to develop. Various individuals may react strongly against bids made by others, particularly if they want to put forward their own bids. In the forming stage members found that the suppression of their own feelings held them back and allowed others to become dominant. In this stage they will probably decide to make their presence felt – as others may be doing this at the same time it is easy to see how conflicts can arise. Some of the behaviours emerging in the early parts of this stage can be summarized as:

- Assertion to the point of aggression
- Strong expression of views
- Frequent challenging of views of others
- Little listening to the views of others
- Lack of collaboration
- Substantial defensiveness
- Challenges for leadership and to the existing leadership
- Use of cliques to obtain power
- Withdrawal by some members
- Development of an emotional state
- Use of formal approaches, eg majority voting to reach decisions

In many ways the group in this stage is forming into three camps – one trying for individual or clique power; one strongly opposing these attempts and pushing forward their own; a third that withdraws from these battles from shyness, confusion or an averse feeling to conflict. The leader is in a difficult position with the possibly formal leadership being challenged strongly from resentment or misunderstanding.

It can be easy for the group to give up any ideas of forming a team at this stage, and indeed many groups never progress beyond this. To progress to the next stage the members must realize the effects their behaviours are having, and the leader must use highly effective techniques to achieve this. What the latter must avoid is trying to move the group on before they show any signs of coming out of the stage. The leader must exert control and guidance to enable progress to occur, but not be over dominant or obvious, and the principal action must be to enable the members to realize the constricting effect of their behaviour. Feedback can create even more conflict, but this action alone will give the members a negative view of themselves and as many controlled reviews as possible should be attempted. Once the strength of the characteristics of this stage start to recede the group can start on the real path to development as a team.

Norming

The development of this stage is a result of and is evidenced by a distinct shift in attitudes to each other and the ways of achieving success. The role of the leader is one of guiding and facilitating, making available every opportunity for the members to take part in activities that will strengthen this development. During the storming stage the members were operating as individuals or as cliques; here the emphasis is beginning to be on mutual aid, the use of each individual's skills and expertise, and a greater degree of tolerance each to the other, particularly the weaker members.

During the norming stage, behaviours are characterized by:

- shared rather than unique leadership
- real listening to the views, opinions and feelings of others
- flexible ways of working and decision making, rather than formal, rigid ones
- preparedness to modify behaviour or ideas to help the team progress
- participation by all, including the shy, reserved, previously uncertain members
- open exchange of ideas and receptiveness to the views of others
- conflicts faced realistically and solved amicably
- high levels of trust between members becoming evident
- tolerance to others' needs, strengths and weaknesses.

Performing

During the norming stage the initial 'group' has gradually changed into a 'team', with the tolerance, trust, close working, etc factors becoming stronger until the team can be readily described as such. The members see themselves as a cohesive team and the behaviour characteristics will include:

- High flexibility of contribution and operation
- High level of mutual trust and openness
- Strong loyalty to the team and each other
- High creativity in problem solving and decision making
- Sharing of leadership according to flexible needs
- Strong relationships but not as cliques
- Acceptance of views of others, but without blind agreement
- Ready resolution of conflict and disagreement
- Flexibility of structure and methods
- High feelings of achievement and success, in both team development and task

The development of a team can also be described in terms of the Johari Window – see Chapter 5 for a full description. In the forming stage, the individuals and the team have a very small Arena, substantial Façade and Blind Spot areas and undetermined Unknown areas. This Johari image continues through the storming stage with the real characteristics of the individuals and team well hidden (the small Arena); a substantial Façade (images presented to hide the real persona); even more substantial blind spots as the conflict clouds all aspects of reality; and no emergence from the Unknown area. The Arena area, the area where characteristics are open to all, increases during the norming stage, when people start to relate more openly towards each other. Consequently the Blind Spot area reduces as, with the new openness and trust, more realistic feedback develops and members are given information on what they have been unaware of themselves. The Façade reduces since there is a lessening need to act a role and to be more oneself, and there is a chance that hitherto unknown information or skills emerge from the Unknown area, again as a result of this openness and mutual working. The Arena is substantial in the final stage – we are whom we are seen to be – with an almost non-existent Façade (there will always be aspects of ourselves about which we do not want others to be aware). Blind Spots reduce even further with very open and extensive feedback. Unknown skills etc can emerge even more easily in this climate of openness, trust, feedback and team spirit.

PROBLEMS ENCOUNTERED IN TEAM DEVELOPMENT

Full and effective progress through the developmental stages of team development can produce, as we have seen, a flexible, self-aware, effective group of people who are mutually supportive in the achievement of task success. The very containment achieved can produce one of the primary problems encountered, even by mature teams. The team can become completely self-contained and inward looking, ignoring the existence and needs of other teams. If this occurs the team has not yet reached full maturity, as one of the principal criteria for an effective team is that it should be able to recognize and link closely with other teams, particularly those with compatible roles and tasks. So a deliberate attempt must be made by the team to forge and maintain these links and so reach full maturity.

Another danger is the over-confidence and comfortable feeling in the relationships that develop within and with the team. What has been described as 'group-think' (all for one and one for all) can develop, resulting in such ideal aspects as individuality and creativity declining. The members do not want to disrupt the harmony that has developed, and this level of team development might even blind the team to the full effectiveness at which they have arrived. Regular team reviews and feedback sessions, occasionally with an external facilitator, can help to avoid this situation, otherwise the team might revert to earlier stages of team development.

Teams or groups of people rarely remain completely stable, with only the original membership. As soon as the membership changes, new members being included, the team starts to revert to an earlier stage, perhaps even as far back as Stage 1. The remaining existing members may feel at Stage 4, but the new member will certainly be having 'forming' feelings, and when the older members realize this they will start to assess their positions *vis-à-vis* the new member. New trusts and openness have to be achieved and the new members and/ or changed team helped again towards Stage 4. This process will be assisted, of course, by the team skills of the existing members who have gone through this process, but only too easily can a 'them and us' attitude develop, the team being destroyed in the process. It helps considerably when changes to the team are announced or envisaged if the existing members plan the processes by which the newcomers can be integrated – these must be deliberate moves as they do not happen accidentally – without any evidence of patronization.

13

Dealing with Difficult People – 1

This chapter:

- gives guidelines on effective approaches to difficult people
- suggests the behaviours you might use in people interactions
- considers techniques and approaches for dealing with difficult situations and people in counselling and appraisal.

WHAT ARE DIFFICULT PEOPLE?

From time to time, everyone in a management or supervisory position will encounter what appear to be problem people. The problems can cover a wide range of situations and part of the manager's responsibilities is to deal with them effectively. In the generally difficult area of training and development for people skills, this particular aspect is probably the hardest to achieve. The initial approach will be use of various techniques that have been seen from experience to work successfully *in a number of cases*. People differ considerably, and an approach that worked with one person is not guaranteed to work with another. Essential in training of this nature is as much practice as possible, using a range of role plays covering a variety of situations. Even with this extensive practice the proof of the pudding will only be in the live environment when real people with real problems have to be dealt with. Training will give the manager some background for these interactions, but they must be approached with considerable care in the real-life situation.

Two particular aspects of dealing with difficult people at work need to be thought about before starting any remedial action or even considering whether to do anything.

1. Many people feel that there are not as many difficult people as there might appear – the majority of these 'difficult' people are normal people reacting negatively to difficult or unsatisfactory *situations*. Consequently if the situation is corrected, the person ceases to be difficult. Of course there are people who are inherently difficult because of personality factors, but (a) we encounter few of these and (b) very little can be done about these under normal conditions.

2. The criterion that must be kept in mind when considering the difficult behaviour of others is first to look at our own behaviour: have we done anything to produce the other's reaction? One significant fact when dealing with people is that *behaviour breeds behaviour* – has anything that we have done contributed to this person's behaviour?

PRE-ACTION CONSIDERATIONS

When you have a difficult person or situation with which to deal, a useful exercise is to quietly consider as many aspects about it as possible. The following list gives some guidance about the areas for consideration.

1. **What is the problem?** Define what is happening, its effect and the extent of the effect it is having on (a) you, (b) others, (c) the work. Many problems when considered in a logical and analytical way frequently turn out not to be problems, or 'problems' about which it is not worth taking any action.

2. **What are the symptoms?** In as much detail as possible, describe how the problem is demonstrated:
   - what is being done that is not acceptable action?
   - what is *not* being done that should be?
   - who is responsible for these actions? Only one person, a number of people, are you included?
   - when is the action being, or not being taken?
   - how did the information come to light?
   - how is the error evident? What effects does it have?
   - how often does the error occur?
   - where does the error occur? Does it have effects in other areas?

3. **Possible causes.** Why do you think, on the evidence you have at the moment, the errors or omissions occur? Consider as many possible causes as you can, but be careful not to come to any conclusion at this stage.

4. **My behaviour or that of others.** Is there anything that I can identify that I or others have done (or not done) that has contributed to the problem? Detail what these factors are or may be.
    - Has any inappropriate behaviour taken place that has caused the other's attitude and behaviour?
    - Have the needs of the 'problem' person been met – training, progression, development, post-training support etc?
    - To what extent has there been communication between the person and me or with others that might have some bearing on the problem?
    - Is it possible to identify an event or period when the problem started and which might be associated with inappropriate behavioural activities – was the person turned down for something in an unsuitable manner, were proposed ideas ignored or rejected out of hand, etc?
5. **Action.** What action should I now take to resolve this situation? The decision may be to take no action, to change specific parameters, to interview others, to interview the problem person. Whatever is decided detailed planning must take place – for example, detailed planning of the interview process.
6. **Obstructions.** Are there any particular problems or obstructions I can identify that will interfere with or make difficult the carrying out of the proposed action? How can I overcome these?

BEHAVIOUR

Behaviour has already been mentioned and in dealing with problem people, as in all people interactions, behaviour – that of the person, your own, or both – is the core of the problem. Remember that, except in rare cases, behaviour will breed behaviour. Treat a person in a humane, gentle, caring manner and there is a much greater likelihood that they will respond in an open way. Treat them coldly or formally and their responses are likely to be uninformative, curt and unfriendly. If someone comes to you bristling with anger and you respond in a like manner the anger will spiral and reach a stage when the 'interaction' will fail; do not react to the anger, whatever the provocation, and gradually the other person will start to cool down and be more amenable to discussion.

Consequently the behavioural temperature of the interaction might be influenced by your behaviour, and you will have to make a positive decision about this; not only what you are going to say, but also how you are going to say it, and ensuring that your verbal and non-verbal behaviours are congruent. Chapter 2 contains descriptions of many of the non-verbal signals that can be used in people interactions and their use in particular behaviours when meeting people are summarized below.

Demonstrating friendliness

> Look the other in the eyes, but do not stare
> Smile whenever appropriate
> Use non-verbal aspects of speech
> Nod your head as they talk
> Hands open and moving occasionally
>   to face
> Lean forward when listening or speaking, but
>   change position occasionally
> Remember the personal proxemic zone

Being considerative

You will note that in the summary above and the one following, for positive non-verbal behaviour in interactions, the signals are very similar for the two approaches. In general these are common behaviours for positive interactions, designed to ensure that you put the other person at ease as much as possible and that you give the strongest indications that you are highly supportive and considerative.

> Look the other in the eyes, but do
>   not stare
> Tilt head slightly as you listen
> Touch chin or nose occasionally
> Use non-verbal aspects of speech
> Lean forward when speaking
> Sit back when listening
> Do not make sudden movements

There may be occasions when you have decided to exhibit negative behaviour, or alternatively you want to ensure that you do not exhibit these. The following behaviour summaries indicate these behaviours.

Defensiveness

Eye contact avoided
Arms crossed
Hands closed
Swivel away from the other
    person
Cross legs with the upper leg
    facing away from the
    other person

These signals should communicate your defensiveness to the other person, who will almost certainly reflect these signals in their own behaviour. As a result the interaction can become defensive and closed with little hope of progress.

Aggression

Maintain continuous eye contact
Stare
Frown
Point finger when making a point
Thump table when making a point
Rub back of neck energetically
Stand while other sits
Walk around making other follow you
    visually
If sitting, lean back in chair with hands
    clasped behind head

When the behaviours summarized above are linked during the interaction with congruent verbal behaviours the other person should be left in no doubt about their reception and the interaction should proceed as you want it to.

SOME SPECIFIC PROBLEMS

It is impossible to define every people problem interaction you will encounter, the variety is very extensive, with many variations even within similar events. Some of the principal problem situations that can occur are described here and the approaches used can be adapted to others.

```
Counselling
Appraisals
Poor performance
Demotivation
Aggression
Grievance
Conflict
Theft
Discipline
Dismissal
```

Two of these interactions will be considered in this chapter – counselling and appraisal. Difficulties are not common, but can arise. The other specific situations will be considered in Chapter 14.

COUNSELLING

This form of manager-staff interaction can often be the most difficult to manage, not necessarily only because of the complexity of the problem brought by the person, but there is also the question of whether managers untrained in psychological counselling should in fact become involved. There are many cases where more harm than good has occurred through bad counselling at the hands of the 'non-professional' counsellor. I do not support this argument in full as one of the responsibilities of managers, within the limits of their capabilities, is for helping, supporting and guiding their staff. Consequently if a member of staff brings a problem (personal or professional) to a manager that manager should accept the plea for help. The techniques of counselling are straightforward and can be learned through training programmes and practised successfully afterwards. The problems arise when the manager is successful and encourages the person to talk about their problems; sometimes allowing them simply to do this is sufficient for the person, who was only seeking a sounding board. But there will be occasions when personal advice is sought, and it is here that the manager, unless fully trained as a counsellor, should be very wary. It is too easy for a manager to be flattered that the problem has been brought to them and react accordingly, but sometimes dangerously.

Counselling situations

A counselling situation arises usually when a member of staff asks the manager if they could have a talk as they have a problem: this problem can be personal, connected with their work (not a technical problem), or a mixture of the two. The manager, unless circumstances do not permit this, should accept the request immediately and invite the person in.

Approaches to helping

One of the decisions a manager can make as part of their intentions for interactions with staff, particularly in counselling situations, is to offer this facility. If this has been done, the manager, in most cases, will at least start the interview knowing what part they are going to play. Four general approaches can be followed:

```
Impose
Propose
Advise
Self-determination
```

Impose. This is the autocratic approach that hardly warrants the title of counselling, but it occurs frequently, particularly with an autocratic manager or organization. There are many pitfalls to the approach:

- the person may resent being *told* what to do
- the imposed solution may be wrong
- acceptance of the solution may be grudging, or not given at all and other actions taken
- dependency on the manager may be encouraged and as a result problems are brought to the manager that could be solved by the person if they thought about them.

On the supportive side, unskilled and inexperienced people might welcome a solution from someone who, presumably, knows all about the problem. Care should be taken by the manager, however, that the pattern does not become permanent and that eventually the people are encouraged to solve their own problems.

Propose. In this approach the manager does not appear superficially to be imposing a solution directly, as several possible solutions can be offered and the problem owner invited to choose the they feel is most appropriate. However, in such cases, the solutions proposed are all acceptable to the manager and take little real account of the needs of the person. Again dependency is encouraged and some people will react against having to choose from an imposed range. A further difficulty is that less experienced people may be concerned about making the 'right' choice. Really this is a backdoor method of imposing a solution without the honesty of showing that this is the case.

Advise. In this approach the manager will listen to the problem and, with honesty, suggest a solution within the limits of their knowledge. At worst the advice is given with the preface 'If I were you, I would. . .' and at best 'I feel the best way of dealing with this is to. . . How do you feel about that?' There is little or no appearance of imposition in these suggestions and the problem owner is given the option of accepting the advice or not. However, members of staff may be reluctant to reject a solution suggested by their boss and simply accept it, albeit a little unwillingly. If the solution fails, they always have the 'out' by saying 'Well, the boss suggested I do it!'

The three approaches described above all include the assumptions that the manager is in possession of all the facts, understands the problem completely, and has to hand all possible solutions. This situation is rare, particularly if the problem owner has withheld some vital information or the interviewing technique has not achieved all that it should have done.

Self-determination. In this approach the solution to the problem and its implementation are placed firmly where they belong – with the problem owner. This is particularly the case with personal problems. In this type of interview the manager will encourage the problem owner to talk about the problem, invite them to suggest possible solutions, discuss these with them, and encourage them to make their own final decision. The atmosphere of this interview is one of the manager being a facilitator, creating an environment in which the problem owner makes their own decisions following exhaustive discussion and clarification. They consequently own their decision and are more likely to be satisfied with its implementation.

This process may be too difficult for some problem owners to take full advantage of, and may need gentle guidance by the manager; but the end decision should be the problem owner's own, or at least appear to be.

An exception to the manager's standing back from specific advice will be in cases where the solution is for the problem owner to go to professional helpers – the manager can then justifiably suggest the most appropriate places for professional advice.

The counselling process

Although counselling is not a difficult people problem as such, a request for a counselling interview can develop into what might be the most difficult people problem a manager might be called upon to deal with. The manager is at a disadvantage from the start, as in most cases they will be unaware what problem is going to be presented to them – the request 'Boss I've got a problem. Can we talk about it?' can be the start of a valuable experience or a nightmare!

Even though every counselling event will differ, the manager is advised to be aware of the process that is most likely to achieve success. The technique is not written in stone, and attitudes must be sufficiently flexible to allow modification as circumstances demand. Training and development programmes in people skills can be very helpful in enabling managers or counsellors to learn the techniques and practise them in the safe atmosphere of the training course. Real learning follows at work when real counselling situations arise.

Many of the techniques and methods have been described elsewhere in this book and can be summarized as a logical process (always retaining flexibility).

Be available
React immediately if possible
Ensure privacy
Make time for the interaction
Use effective seating
Ease into the discussion
Open with seeking factual information
Move on to 'feelings' level when appropriate
Use effective questioning techniques
Listen
Accept silences
Seek information about action taken so far
Seek possible solutions
Discuss a range of solutions
Seek solution decision
Summarize

Most of these steps are self-explanatory, although a comment on some items can be helpful.

Using effective seating. Avoid an 'across the desk' orientation, as the desk can create a barrier that can inhibit feelings emerging. More appropriate for a semi-formal situation is across the corner of the desk or, in a very informal case, side by side.

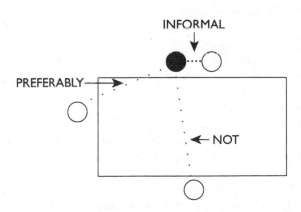

Figure 13.1   *Seating options*

Accepting silences. A silence, particularly after a question to the problem owner, does not necessarily mean they are not going to answer or do not want to answer. More often than not they are thinking about what they can and/or want to say, so sit out a reasonable amount of silence before questioning it. After all, your question may not have been understandable, but it is not wise to ask bluntly whether they have understood it as, this may seem patronizing.

Summarizing. The manager can summarize at the end of the interview:

- what has been discussed
- what solutions have been considered
- what solutions have been agreed
- what the action is to be taken, by whom and by when.

Rather than the manager describe the summary, in order to consolidate the results in the mind of the problem owner they can be invited to summarize, supported by the manager.

APPRAISALS

This is another people interaction that essentially is not a problem, but it can so easily become one. There are a number of different approaches to appraisal interviews, but the basic format is usually as follows.

---

1. Agree a date and time with the appraisee
2. Issue a self-preparation document to the appraisee for pre-completion
3. Complete the report form
4. (Give the appraisee a pre-interview copy of the report)
5. Meet the appraisee to discuss:
   (a) Past performance and achievement of objectives
   (b) Agreement on objectives for next year and methods of achievement
   (c) training and development necessary
6. Agree and produce action plan and copy to both appraiser and appraisee

---

According to the organization and the appraisal scheme it operates, some of the above may not be included in the format, particularly items 2 and 4, and some schemes may have additional items.

However, whatever the scheme, little difficulty ever arises when the report on the person is good and the future development or performance is readily agreed. The problem situations arise when the appraisal report is (a) a bad one and (b) the appraisee does not accept the report given.

On too many such occasions problems arise because of the manner in which the 'bad news' is presented, usually starting with 'Well Fred, this year hasn't been a good one for you has it? You made of a mess of all sorts of things.' This approach frequently produces the response 'I can't agree with that. I think I've done well – what about so and so. . .'

This approach has three obvious faults:

1. the appraisee is immediately attacked with negative issues
2. the negative issues are not specified
3. the tone is a patronizing, autocratic, reprimanding one.

A start of this nature does not bode well for the interview and, unless the interviewer is very skilled at retrieving situations, it will finish unsuccessfully, both parties feeling frustrated at the lack of progress.

One possible approach that is likely to succeed to a greater extent could follow this pattern.

1.	Describe the purpose and pattern of the interview
2.	Discuss the appraisee's tasks and roles in the year under review
3.	Seek appraisee's views of this year's work
4.	Comment favourably (and sincerely) on jobs well done
5.	If the negative events are not raised, raise them by seeking appraisee's views on how he/she performed
6.	Discuss response to obtain agreement on actual achievement and how this might have been improved
7.	Discuss coming year's objectives and tasks and seek views on how success might be achieved
8.	Seek appraisee's views on training and development needed
9.	Agree and summarize objectives, tasks and development
10.	Agree interim review meeting
11.	Produce and copy action plan

Obviously within this skeletal plan not only what is done is important, but equally, if not more so, is *how* it is done, *how* the comments are expressed by the appraiser and what words are used. Rarely should an appraiser start with 'I think. . .', rather the words should reflect 'How do/did you feel about. . .?', 'What do you think you could do to. . .?' and so on. These approaches turn the appraisal interaction into almost a counselling interview and the behaviours used by the appraiser can reflect those suggested in the counselling approach described above.

It would be naïve to suggest that this 'softly, softly' approach would work in every case. At times the appraisee will simply refuse to accept that they have performed poorly. The appraiser, invoking all the evidence that must have been collected previously, must then show the other that their opinion is erroneous and try to obtain their acceptance of the facts. Even then, there may be rare cases when refusal continues and in such cases the appraiser must take a draconian approach – however, this interview must be considered a failure and the interviewer must assess very carefully their own part and behaviour in the interview.

It is possibly more difficult to deal with problem people in situations where problems are not expected, such as in the counselling and appraisal events described above. But there are frequently more specific problem people with whom the manager or supervisor has to deal, and these are considered in the following chapter.

14

Dealing with Difficult People – 2

This chapter:

- describes specific people problem situations and gives guidance in dealing with: poor performers; demotivated people; aggressive people; grievance situations; reprimand, disciplinary and dismissal situations.

Not every interaction with a difficult person or situation arises during an event, such as an appraisal interview, and has to be dealt with 'on the hoof'. Many people interactions of a difficult nature can be anticipated so, instead of knowing how to interact immediately, the skills in these cases include a pre-knowledge of the problem and how to cope with this type of problem. The cases that follow are of this second type.

POOR PERFORMERS

Every manager or supervisor will at some time in their career encounter someone who does not perform to the necessary standards. These poor performance problems can exhibit themselves in one or more of:

- performance of the required task(s)
- interpersonal problems with individuals or the group/team as a whole and/or personal behaviour problems.

In general, problems related to task performance are most readily remedied and a series of steps towards achievement is recommended. Questions to resolve include the following:

Is there in fact a problem and is it related to the work? It is not unknown for a manager to complain that somebody is/gives them a problem, whereas the truth is that the poor performance is caused by circumstances.

- Has the person's work changed so recently that they cannot yet have achieved competence standards?
- Are the errors or omissions tasks that are not included in the person's job description? If this is the case, whose responsibility was it to vary the description?
- Have any changes put the work level beyond the capabilities of the person?
- In the previous case, or in a more general sense, has the person received adequate and sufficient training and development to enable them to perform their (new) job?
- Are you seeking too much from someone whom you might have engaged at a particular level? You may not have realized that you have been asking so much without taking other steps to ensure success.
- Is the person, if all the previous aspects have been considered, still underperforming? Are you sure that they are capable of achieving what you are asking?

Is the problem one of interpersonal behaviour? Most of these cases occur when the person is capable of performing the work but they fail to perform appropriately because they do not wish to do so, or perhaps are unable, behaviourally, to do so. The questions to ask in this case include:

- Is this unwillingness to perform of long standing, or has it started recently?
- Can you identify any event or incident that may have triggered a changed attitude?
- Has the person's job role been changed against their preferences?
- Has a colleague been promoted with the presently poorly performing worker feeling aggrieved that the promotion should have gone to them?
- Were changes that have affected the person within the group made without any personal introduction of the changes – perhaps the person was absent when the relevant meeting was held, but was there subsequent failure to bring them up to date?
- Have bad feelings developed for some reason between the person and another individual or the rest of the group?

- May the poor performance be due to external factors – poor personal health or that of a close family member, domestic or financial problems?

Remedial action

Whichever of the reasons listed above, or any others, is the cause of the poor performance, the necessary action by the manager is to meet the person to:

- determine the reasons
- agree methods of achieving improvement.

The reason for the poor performance will direct the mode of the interview. Obviously the poor performance will have been observed and examples retained as 'evidence'. The first interactive step will be to determine why the performance is occurring. In most cases an interview of this nature will develop into a form of the counselling interview described earlier, and a useful format could be:

1. Agree a mutually convenient time and place to meet, giving the person advance warning about the nature of the meeting. Some people disagree with forewarning, suggesting that this gives the person time to construct a plausible, but untrue story. This may be so, but the converse argument is that it is not humane to spring on a person what almost amounts to a disciplinary interview.
2. Start the interview by confirming that the principal purpose of the interaction is to help the person to develop and improve and so enhance their chance of progression in the organization and that, at that stage, it is not a disciplinary interview. It may of course develop into a first stage of this procedure, but at this early point in the interaction an open mind must be retained.
3. Describe the circumstances that have led to your calling this meeting, quoting some of the evidence (retain some for possible later use) and explaining how the reduced (rarely say 'poor') performance is harming:
   - the person – their status and future development
   - their colleagues
   - the required work
   - the organization.
4. Seek statements by the person about reasons why the performance has deteriorated to the extent observed. It will be necessary in this

stage to use every aspect of effecting questioning as described earlier to obtain all the information the person is willing to disclose. If the person will not disclose sufficient information to give a reasonable cause for the poor performance, the question of converting the interview to a reprimand must be considered.

5. If the reasons given are ones that can be remedied, and the performer is willing to do so, a discussion should follow on the action to be taken. This may be by the performer themselves, by the performer in conjunction with others (including the manager), or by the manager alone. Care must be taken that the manager does not try to solve a problem (as in the counselling situation) for which he or she is not professionally qualified, restricting advice perhaps to information about where the person might go to seek professional help.

    The solutions will become obvious from the root causes of the problem, and in most cases can be remedied by local action or reference to training and development.

6. Interpersonal or behavioural problems will be more difficult to resolve, involving:

    ■ the need to help the person towards self-motivation
    ■ discussing the person's *feelings* and means of enhancing these
    ■ agreeing a method of resolving a disagreement
    ■ agreeing interpersonal or assertiveness developmental training
    ■ discussing the personal problems that are the cause of the work problems and agreeing action to try to resolve these. (These are certainly cases where the only solution is to have the poor performer take their problem to a relevant professional.)

It is common in interviews of this nature to learn that the person is completely unaware of the problems and the effect their behaviour is having on others. Considerable care must be taken in explaining examples of these since, in effect, you are criticizing a person not a job. Perhaps in cases such as this, more than in direct work cases, the person may reject the comments and it can be very difficult *persuading* them to see the reality.

Some golden rules

Some golden rules for interviewing poor performers (also useful to remember in other interactions) include the following:

Obtain as much concrete evidence as possible before taking any action

Always interview in privacy

Ensure that the interviewee realizes that the purpose of the meeting is to help

Only promise changes – environment, resources – if these are possible

Be aware of the issues of sex, age, race, disability and age differences

Avoid comments on a person's *personality*, stick to behaviour and its effects

Ensure that the person understands the consequences of their actions

Examine at all times your own value judgements and reasons for taking action

Always mean what you say and what you will do

DEMOTIVATED PEOPLE

People may not be motivated as fully as you would want or expect, and commonly lose their motivation as time goes by, usually resulting in poor (or, at best, just satisfactory) performance. A significant degree of motivation is essential in effective operation, but it can be a perplexing issue for the manager faced by reduced motivation or its total absence.

Some of the models of motivation were discussed in Chapter 5, principally those of Maslow and Herzberg, but the main consideration to bear in mind is that motivation is self-generated and you cannot motivate people to work. All you can do is to ensure that all Herzberg's hygiene factors are present so that the people concerned have the opportunity to self-motivate.

Some of the many causes of demotivation are:

Inadequate pay
Poor working conditions
Work of a temporary nature
Lack of job security
Poor working atmosphere
Low personal status
Inadequate skills
Low chance of progression
Inappropriate organization culture
Ineffective management and supervision
Poor interpersonal relationships

Most of the possible causes listed above speak for themselves, but resolution of the problems can be far from simple or straightforward, and you may have to accept that some cannot be resolved or require long-term action. For example, if the culture of the organization is oppressive, over-restraining and excessively formal the employees have to accept these constraints and work within them. At lower levels in the organization motivation can be encouraged by managers who are willing to offer a better atmosphere in their local unit, although the overall 'gloom and doom' can still be present.

Pay can be a problem if there are pay norms for specific groups and to change the pay structure for one, demotivated person, could start an organizational or national problem. There can sometimes be ways round this problem if the manager has the power to develop roles of responsibility for which higher pay would be attracted – this of course assumes that the person concerned is worthy of this action.

Herzberg suggested in his model that demotivators, such as those listed, reduce motivation if they exist; but correcting them does not necessarily mean that motivation will result. What is additionally necessary are positive motivational factors that enable the people concerned to motivate themselves. Some typical motivation factors are:

Achievement and further achievement
Recognition
Progress and advancement
Satisfying work
Responsibility for self and others

Achievement

Demotivation soon appears if individuals do not achieve the task objectives they have set or that have been set for them, particularly if successive tasks fail. People need personal success to continue to the next task, with the motivated attitude that they are going to continue to succeed. Perhaps they are performing work that is beyond their skill level, or they require training to succeed. At times objectives are set that are too far beyond possible achievement – an objective must stretch the person, yet still be achievable. Or the task can be broken down into a number of smaller tasks, each more easily attainable that the task in its entirety – the 'elephant diet' factor!

Recognition

When tasks and objectives are achieved the individual gains a lot of personal satisfaction that continues their motivation. However, if this is a permanent state and the achievement is never given recognition – praise or even awareness – demotivation starts to set in: 'I may as well not do this as I'm never thanked for it!' In most cases the solution is simple, via a 'thank you' or 'well done' that lets the person know they have been *seen* to perform the task well. The usual excuse is 'Oh, they know I'm grateful. I don't need to keep on saying thank you' – but people want this. A balance has to be struck: too frequent thanks starts to sound insincere and patronizing (both demotivators), so one approach might be a very simple recognition for routine achievements and something more special when a substantial task has been achieved.

Progress and advancement

Many people (though not all) at work are looking to progress upwards in the job and the organization, usually in the form of promotion, although it can be to more responsible tasks or jobs. Not everybody can be promoted, or is suitable, but some arrangements must be made for the different levels of possible progression. Otherwise, particularly if the individual sees colleagues progressing while he or she stays still, demotivation sets in.

Satisfying work

Investigations and research have shown, perhaps surprisingly, that money is not the principal factor that gives people satisfaction at work. Even those who profess that they only work so that they can earn sufficient money with which to live soon start questioning their job satisfaction and may seek a more challenging one, hopefully with more money! Is the 'Monday morning' syndrome too strong among your staff? Apart from workaholics, most people after the weekend break have some reluctance to return to work, but if this attitude continues throughout the week you have a demotivated staff whose work is probably not satisfying. Satisfied workers will also be the ones who come forward with new and creative ideas to produce improvements.

Responsibility for self and others

The natural desire for personal advancement was mentioned above: not everybody wants to be the chief executive, but advancement usually brings with it a greater responsibility for one's own actions and frequently those of others. Responsibility also brings with it a strong measure of self-esteem and a desire to progress even further, in addition to an altruistic feeling of wanting to help others to achieve.

AGGRESSIVE PEOPLE

Aggression is the opposite of non-assertiveness and is a demonstration that the aggressive person is only concerned with their own opinions and actions, and has no thoughts against violating, ignoring or dominating the rights of others. There are very few occasions when aggression can be resolved by counter-aggression: usually the effect is an escalation of the initial aggression. It is difficult to take a softly, softly approach when faced by someone with an aggressive manner, but if you do not know the reason for the attitude, this is the approach you must take.

One possibly effective way of handling situations such as this is to:

1. Take a deep breath, but do not take up a similarly aggressive stance.
2. Ask, calmly, what the reasons are for the approach and listen, carefully and obviously.
3. Probe to ensure full understanding and a statement of the complete set of facts.

4. Reflect the position as you see it from what has been said – this lets the person know you have been listening, have understood all that they wished to say, and that they have said everything they wanted to say.
5. In many cases, the atmosphere will become more reasonable if the 'aggressor' is allowed to talk out a lot of the aggressive feelings.
6. If the problem involves others or tasks that require investigation, suggest a temporary adjournment so that any other people concerned can be met and/or you can make enquiries.
7. If the aggressor's problem is justified, agree action with them to resolve the problem.
8. If the aggressor's complaints are clearly unjustified, let them know that this is your opinion and that continued aggression will not help towards a resolution of the situation. It may also help, as suggested above, to let them continue talking as they may talk themselves out of their aggressive attitude, particularly if they realize their attitude is getting them nowhere.
9. If all else fails and the aggression is still as strong, suggest a cooling-off period before meeting again to discuss the problem more rationally

Obviously not all aggressive situations will be resolved using these suggestions. Particularly if after the cooling-off period suggested in (9) and your investigations as in (6) the aggressive attitude remains, you may have to use a final managerial draconian measure – this must obviously be a last resort, but it is a possibility. It does not necessarily mean that you have failed in your dealing with the people problem.

GRIEVANCE SITUATIONS

Frequently this type of people interaction is synonymous with the aggression situation described above and can be dealt with in the same manner. This is little different from the general approach to grievance situations, but without the animosity. Essential in any organization is (a) a grievance procedure known by all members of the organization and (b) the facilities for grievances to be aired to the relevant person (usually the manager or supervisor). Some problems can occur when the grievance is against the person to whom grievances would normally be taken, but effective procedures include measures to cover these contingencies. A summary of the action that might be taken for effective resolution when a grievance is brought to you would include:

Wherever possible agree to an immediate interview
    when requested
Ensure full privacy and allocation of time
Ask the grievee to state their grievance as fully as possible
Listen carefully and make notes of the grievance and
    its effects
Probe to ensure your full understanding
Probe to ensure the emergence of the complete set of facts
Reflect the grievance as you see it and seek agreement of
    the facts
Always encourage the grievee to talk, so defusing any aggression
Adjourn if others or tasks require investigation
If the grievance is justified, agree action to resolve the problem
If the grievance is unjustified give your reasons and seek
    agreement
If agreement cannot be reached, suggest a 'cooling-off'
    period and a later meeting
If agreement still cannot be reached, ask for the grievance to be
    stated in writing for consideration by a higher level in
    accordance with agreed procedures

Some golden rules

If you, or the organization are at fault, accept this and apologize
Don't try to justify your position
Avoid giving excuses – they often sound lame and are rarely
    accepted
Accept that you are the person the grievee should be talking
    to – if this is so
Don't interrupt the person in full flow – they will only start
    over again or become aggressive
Listen to all the facts before reaching a conclusion
Sympathize without accepting the grievance or being disloyal
    to people or the organization

REPRIMAND, DISCIPLINE AND DISMISSAL

These are people problem situations and interviews with which managers and supervisors tell me they are least comfortable and frequently find embarrassing. Most people do not like having to reprimand others, particularly a member of your staff whom you have known for some time, but situations requiring this action do occur and skills for coping with them must be developed. Organizations are required to have set procedures for dealing with discipline problems, but of course the people behaviour within the resulting interviews can be varied to some extent.

Discipline can include:

- a simple, on the spot ticking-off for a minor misdemeanour
- an interview, although still relatively informal and not within the official procedure
- the full disciplinary interview.

Employment law concerned with discipline, particularly that leading to dismissal, does not prescribe any definitive procedure, but recommends the procedure be written and available to all employees:

- stating to whom it refers
- outlining the actions that are to be taken
- specifying who has authority to take action
- giving individuals the right to be represented at an interview (trade union representative or 'soldier's friend')
- explaining that, except in cases of gross misconduct (defined) dismissal is not an action in the case of a first breach
- ensuring that individuals are given in writing an explanation of penalties imposed or action that has to be taken
- providing a right of appeal at any stage and detailing the procedure for this.

Further recommendations where the offence is sufficiently serious to justify the action include:

- an oral warning for a first offence
- a written warning following a formal interview for a second offence
- dismissal for a third offence.

However, the principal purpose of discipline approaches is to try to achieve improvement in the future, rather than simply looking at historical actions. Consequently, unless it is obvious that the problem is very serious and unlikely to be resolved simply, informal interviews are likely to succeed in most cases. Whatever the informality or formality of the interview, in order that the interaction reaches a successful conclusion, specific stages of planning and implementation should be followed.

Before the interview

1. Check the facts of the breach of procedure or other action requiring reprimand or discipline.
2. Check the required standards of competence or behaviour.
3. Decide whether an informal reprimand is required or the formal discipline procedure should be followed.
4. In most cases, start a record of the event and action taken.
5. Inform the person that action is to be taken and agree a date and time for the initial meeting.
6. Inform the person of their rights under the discipline procedures.

The reprimand interview

This is the type of discipline action between the informal ticking-off and the formal discipline procedure, although it can eventually form part of the latter. It should be viewed more as a counselling or rectifying action than one of discipline. A format for an interview of this nature could be:

- ensure privacy in a room suitable for the purpose
- consider the value of a non-confrontational seating arrangement
- explain to the person being reprimanded the reason for and the facts of the situation
- seek the person's views on the reasons why the breach occurred
- listen carefully
- probe for uncertainties, evasions and omissions
- ensure that all possible information emerges and that the person is satisfied they have had the opportunity to have their say
- as a result of the emergence of perhaps previously unknown facts and information concerned with the breach, decide and agree with the person what action is to be taken

- agree a review date to consider the agreed actions
- maintain an informal record of the interview.

The foregoing format assumes that the interview progresses in a favourable manner and the person agrees that the breach has occurred. There may be occasions when the person will disagree with the stated breach, although these may suggest that you have not effectively investigated the breach before taking the interview. The action will then depend on the extent to which you are absolutely certain that your evidence is full and accurate. If you are convinced of this, the interview should be terminated to be resumed as a formal, disciplinary interview. Otherwise, the person might show you that you were not in full possession of the facts, or there were mitigating circumstances – it may be that the further process can be ignored.

The discipline interview

This description refers to the action to be taken in cases of serious offence that could lead to dismissal or perhaps lesser disciplinary action. The start of the process can be as described in the reprimand interview, but it is even more essential that the interviewer is in possession of the full facts and is convinced of their completeness and accuracy. If this is not the case, no action should be taken, as a range of problems could arise from a failure to demonstrate the breach. This first interview is the oral warning when the breach has been confirmed and the person is required to agree action to avoid repetition. It is essential that a record of the interview, the process and the action agreed is made, as accurately and as fully as possible.

Even at this stage, the interviewer's background feelings should be of potential support and employee improvement rather than disciplinary action, and every support should be given to try to ensure non-repetition.

If, following this first interview, improvement or rectification is not observed over the period agreed the second disciplinary interview in the process should take place.

The second discipline interview

By this stage the situation has become much more serious as a result of the failure of the person to benefit from the almost informal warning of the first meeting, and the attitude will now be much more formal. Even so, although we are now in a discipline situation, background feelings of the interviewer should still be those of improvement rather than looking to probable dismissal. However, the person must be left in no doubt about the seriousness of the situation and the possible effects of their actions. The pattern of the interview, following all the pre-interview investigations and production of an effective environment, will be very similar to the first.

- State that there has been a repetition of the breach or no other improvement, depending on the events, and that this is a formal discipline interview.
- Ask for the person's comments and reasons for failure to improve.
- If there are no new factors to take into account, give a warning to the person to the effect that if improvement does not occur, dismissal will result.
- Issue the warning in writing, particularly stating a date when the case will be reviewed to confirm what has happened.
- Write up the record of the interview.

The third discipline interview

This interview might, depending on the organization's code of practice, be a second written warning interview, but might equally be dispensed with. In the latter case the interview becomes one of dismissal, and is the end of the road, the person being deemed to have been given sufficient opportunity and support to rectify breaches or improve.

If the event is one leading to dismissal of the employee, this end of the road viewpoint must be kept in mind, as action has virtually been determined. The process is relatively simple and involves the interviewer:

- summarizing to the person the actions that have taken place, the issuing of warnings and their failure to rectify or improve
- reminding them that they were informed the result of these failures would lead to dismissal and that is now the case
- asking them if they have any further comments to make (there should be no surprises at this stage)
- issuing the required dismissal notice
- terminating the interview and writing up the process record.

If you are to be involved in the disciplinary process you should make early contact with the personnel department of your organization, who will give you guidance on (a) the activities in which you should engage, (b) your responsibility for certain actions and (c) your authority in the discipline and dismissal processes.

Dismissal

The discipline situations described above are ones where the person has not committed what is described as gross misconduct and the discipline action, basically one of improvement rather that punishment, extends over a period of time during which the offender is given the opportunity to remedy their breaches of omission or commission. Unless the person is particularly awkward during this process these interactions can be at a non-aggressive, even friendly level, and many have a positive outcome.

However, in any manager's career, where he or she has the authority to 'hire and fire' or where these responsibilities are delegated to them by senior management or personnel departments, drastic and potentially traumatic situations can arise. A substantial amount of employment legislation is in force to protect both the employee and employer, and all managers should be fully aware of their responsibilities, actions and rights, particularly as they relate to serious discipline and dismissal situations.

There are two essential requirements to be met.

1. The information about employment protection must be made available to all employees, usually by exhibiting a notice in a prominent place or places, including those requirements of the *organization* additional to the minimum statutory ones.
2. Before discipline or dismissal action is taken the manager must be completely clear and convinced about the facts of the case.

Certain misdemeanours warrant instant dismissal, without recourse to the more extended discipline procedures described earlier, but in these cases the manager must be absolutely certain of the ground before proceeding. If you cannot quote chapter and verse, and go ahead with the dismissal, you may be leaving the organization open to many problems, principally appeals to the statutory authorities under unfair or wrongful dismissal. Particular care should be taken with employees with more than two years employment, as these workers are covered completely by the employment legislation. The success of such a challenge can result in reinstatement rights and financial penalties.

The more common circumstances of dismissal can include:

- gross misconduct, which can include violence towards fellow-workers or more senior people
- drinking and/or drug taking that renders the person incapable of performing their duties or jeopardizes safety in the workplace; in

some organizations there are additional sanctions of dismissal if the person has simply taken alcohol or drugs during their hours of work

- serious disruption of staff interrelationships
- disregard of health and safety rules, thereby seriously affecting the rights of other workers
- gross insubordination
- financial irregularities

In many cases the information available is not straightforward or easily obtainable, but in summary dismissal this is essential. Usually the event that leads to the dismissal is not an isolated one – such an event would more probably lead to an investigatory interview linked with a discipline situation – and, unless the act is not extremely serious, may be dealt with by obtaining direct evidence over a relevant period and recording this evidence. Many of the terms used in these types of situations sound like those used in courts of law, and in fact this may be a useful parallel as subsequent reference to appeal tribunals and courts are not unknown.

The dismissal interview

When an incident has occurred that warrants summary dismissal, prior action must include:

Confirmation that the rules were available
   to the person
What action has been taken over any similar
   incident with this employee?
What records are available?
Are you *fully* aware of the facts and evidence
   of the event?
Do you need witnesses and are they available?

At the actual interview:

> State the facts and that this is leading to immediate
> suspension with the possibility that it will lead to
> dismissal
>
> Ask the person if they wish anyone to be present
>
> Ask the person if they have anything to say about
> the offence
>
> If there appear to be some justifiable grounds, obtain
> full information and adjourn the interview for
> further investigation
>
> If the case is proven, either issue the dismissal notice
> or refer to the person with authority to dismiss

Five points to bear in mind at all times when dismissal is the issue are:

> 1. Evidence must be direct and not based
>   on hearsay
> 2. Do not be drawn into argument
> 3. Do not react to the anger that usually occurs
> 4. Make no comments related to sex, race, disability
> 5. In the face of unjustified disagreement, continue
>   action

Discipline and dismissal situations are the most difficult, awkward and embarrassing people situations in which managers and supervisors can find themselves, but their resolution must not be avoided. Lines of responsibility should be clear and there should be no question of delegation or relegation of these responsibilities. Even in serious cases every attempt should be made to resolve the situation in a positive manner, but you must be prepared to take the more drastic types of action if resolution is not otherwise possible.

People managers find that most of their dealings with people are pleasant, enjoyable and satisfying, but they must be prepared to deal with the eventualities described in this chapter and many other people problems. You should always be sure of your ground before taking any action and above all, when you ask the other person to comment, *listen*.

Many people problem situations that arise can be avoided by a humane attitude and following some of the advice and guidance given in the preceding chapters – good people relationships are not easy but are well worthwhile and can be extremely satisfying, in addition to making your managerial life easier!

Suggested Reading

Few books that cover a range of related subjects can deal with each subject in great detail – this book is no exception. However, there are published titles that deal with more singular subjects in considerable detail and the reader is recommended to these in particular cases. Included in the references are publications containing practical activities directly related to the subject: these are essential inclusions in any training programme involving learning about handling people problems. The subjects are also included in more general communication, training and management publications as separate chapters or sections. The publications are listed in sections that relate to the various topics covered, although there will invariably be a certain amount of overlap.

Appraisal

Denham, Wendy and Jestico, Jane (1993), *50 Activities for Appraisal Training*, Gower.

Fisher, Martin (1995), *Performance Appraisals*, Kogan Page.

Fletcher, C (1993), *Appraisal – routes to improved performance*, IPM.

Hudson, Howard (1992), *The Perfect Appraisal*, Century Business.

McCallum, Carol (1992), *How to Design and Introduce an Appraisal Training System*, Kogan Page.

Moon, Philip (1993), *Appraising your Staff*, Kogan Page.

Prior, John (ed) (1994), *Handbook of Training and Development*, Gower.

Slater, John and Packard, Peter (1988), *The Skills of Appraisal (a training package)*, Gower.

Assertiveness

Back, Ken and Back, Kate (1982), *Assertiveness at Work*, McGraw-Hill.

Bishop, Sue (1995), *Assertiveness Skills Training: A sourcebook of activities*, Kogan Page.

Bishop, Sue (1996), *Develop your Assertiveness*, Kogan Page

Gillen, Terry (1996), *Assertiveness for Managers*, Gower.

Kelly, Colleen (1979), *Assertion Training*, University Associates.

Seifert, Lucy (1994), *Training for Assertiveness*, Gower (includes 40 assert-iveness activities).

Stubbs, David R (1985), *How to use Assertiveness at Work*, Gower.

Behaviour

Argyle, Michael (1967), *The Psychology of Interpersonal Behaviour*, Penguin.

Bales, R F (1950), *Interaction Process Analysis*, Addison-Wesley.

Blake, Robert R and Mouton, Jane S (1978), *The New Managerial Grid*, Gulf.

Honey, Peter and Mumford, Alan (1992), *The Manual of Learning Styles*, Peter Honey Publications.

Kolb, DA, Rubin, I M and McIntyre, J M (1974), *Organizational Psychology – An experiential approach*, Prentice Hall.

Maslow, Abraham H (1954), *Motivation and Personality*, Harper.

Prior, John (ed) (1994), *Handbook of Training and Development*, Gower.

Rackham, Neil and Morgan, Terry (1977), *Behaviour Analysis in Training*, McGraw-Hill.

Rackham, Neil and Honey, Peter (1971), *Developing Interactive Skills*, Wellens.

Russell, Tim (1994), *Effective Feedback Skills*, Kogan Page.

Skinner, B F (1974), *About Behaviourism*, Alfred A Knopf.

Coaching

Baston, Rob (1991), *Delegation Skills (A one-day workshop package)*, Kogan Page.

Buckley, Roger and Caple, Jim (1996), *One-to-one Training and Coaching Skills*, Kogan Page.

Kalinauckas, Paul and King, Helen (1994), *Coaching: Realising the potential*, IPD.

Kinlaw, Dennis C (1997), *Coaching: Winning strategies for individuals and teams*, Gower.

Lowe, Phil (1994), *Coaching and Counselling Skills (A one-day workshop package)*, Kogan Page.

MacLennan, Nigel (1995), *Coaching and Mentoring*, Gower.

Meggison, David and Boydell, Tom (1979), *A Manager's Guide to Coaching*, BACIE.

Parsloe, Eric (1992), *Coaching, Mentoring and Assessing*, Kogan Page.

Parsloe, Eric (1995), *Coaching to Handle Customers' Problems*, Fenman.

Prior, John (ed) (1994), *Handbook of Training and Development*, Gower.

Salisbury, Frank S (1994), *Developing Managers as Coaches*, McGraw-Hill.

Whittaker, Mike and Cartwright, Ann (1997), *32 Activities on Coaching and Mentoring*, Gower.

Communication

Argyle, M (1988), *Bodily Communication*, Routledge.
Carter, Wendy (1993), *Communication Skills (A one-day workshop package)*, Kogan Page.
Dimmick, Sally (1995), *Successful Communication through NLP*, Gower.
Morris, Desmond (1978), *Manwatching: A field guide to human behaviour*, Triad Books.
Pease, Allan (1981), *Body Language*, Sheldon Press.
Prior, John (ed) (1994), *Handbook of Training and Development*, Gower.
Scholes, Eileen (ed) (1997), *Handbook of Internal Communication*, Gower.

General

Edwards, Martin (1993), *Dismissal Law: A practical guide for managers*, Kogan Page.
Rae, Leslie (1992), *Guide to In-company Training Methods*, Gower.
Rae, Leslie (1995), *Techniques of Training*, Gower.
Rae, Leslie (1996), *Using Activities in Training and Development*, Kogan Page.
Rae, Leslie (1997), *Planning and Designing Training Programmes*, Gower.

Investors in People

Taylor, Peter and Thackwray, Bob (1996), *Investors in People Explained*, Kogan Page.
Taylor, Peter and Thackwray, Bob (1997), *Managing for Investors in People*, Kogan Page.

Mentoring

Clutterbuck, David and Megginson, David (1997), *Mentoring in Action: A practical guide for managers*, Kogan Page.
MacLennan, Nigel (1995), *Coaching and Mentoring*, Gower.
Parsloe, Eric (1992), *Coaching, Mentoring and Assessing*, Kogan Page.
Prior, John (ed) (1994), *Handbook of Training and Development*, Gower.
Whittaker, Mike and Cartwright, Ann (1997), *32 Activities on Coaching and Mentoring*, Gower.

People skills

Allan, Jane (1989), *How to Solve People Problems*, Kogan Page.

Bailey, Roy (1991), *50 Activities for Developing Counselling Skills*, Gower.

Bishop, Sue (1997), *The Complete Guide to People Skills*, Gower.

Bishop, Sue and Taylor, David (1991), *50 Activities for Interpersonal Skills Training*, Gower.

Burnard, Philip (1992), *Interpersonal Skills Training: A sourcebook of activities for trainers*, Kogan Page (includes 110 activities suitable for interpersonal skills training).

Burnard, Philip (1996), *Counselling Skills Training: A resource of activities for trainers*, Kogan Page.

Clinard, Helen H (1985), *Winning Ways to Succeed with People*, Gulf.

Edenborough, Robert (1996), *Effective Interviewing: A handbook of skills, techniques and applications*, Kogan Page.

Gratus, Jack (1991), *Sharpen up your Interviewing*, Mercury.

Honey, Peter (1992), *Problem People and how to Manage Them*, IPM.

Honey, Peter (1996), *Face to Face Skills*, Gower.

Hussey, David (1992), *How to Motivate People (A one-day workshop package)*, Kogan Page.

Lowe, Phil (1994), *Coaching and Counselling Skills (A one-day workshop package)*, Kogan Page.

Lowe, Phil (1994), *Recruitment and Interviewing Skills (A one-day workshop package)*, Kogan Page.

MacKay, Ian (1993), *35 Checklists For Human Resource Management*, Gower.

MacLennan, Nigel (1996), *Counselling for Managers*, Gower.

Prior, John (ed) (1994), *Handbook of Training and Development*, Gower.

Rae, Leslie (1988), *The Skills of Interviewing*, Gower.

Rae, Leslie (1985), *The Skills of Human Relations Training*, Gower.

Stewart, Jacqueline and Couper, David (1993), *50 Activities for Developing People Skills*, Gower.

Stewart, Jacqueline and Couper, David (1995), *38 Activities for Handling Difficult Situations*, Gower.

Tidman, Peter and Slater, Lloyd (1992), *Tidman's Media Interview Techniques*, McGraw-Hill.

Walmsley, Hilary (1994), *Counselling Techniques for Managers*, Kogan Page.

Williams, Beverley (1997), *Managing Tricky Situations at Work (18 activities)*, Fenman.

Role plays

Couper, David and Stewart, Jacqueline (1993), *25 Role Plays for Developing Counselling Skills*, Gower.

Maier, Solem and Maier (1975), *The Role Play Technique*, University Associates.

Ments, Morry van (1994), *The Effective Use of Role Play*, Kogan Page.

Smith, Joseph (1995), *People Problems at Work: 40 role plays for managers*, Fenman.

Turner, David (1992), *Role Plays: A sourcebook of activities for trainers*, Kogan Page (60 role plays covering negotiation, appraisal, discipline, grievance, managing people at work).

Teamworking

Adair, John, (1986), *Effective Teambuilding*, Gower.

Allan, John (1994), *25 Team Management Training Sessions*, Gower.

Belbin, R Meredith (1981), *Management Teams: Why they succeed or fail*, Heinemann.

Clark, Neil (1994), *Team Building – A practical guide for trainers*, McGraw-Hill.

David, John *et al* (1993), *Successful Team Building*, Kogan Page.

Eales-White, Rupert (1995), *Building your Team*, Kogan Page.

Lewis, Ralph (1995), *Teambuilding Skills (A one-day workshop package)*, Kogan Page.

Margerison, C J and McCann, D J (1984), *The Team Management Index*, MCB University Press.

Margerison, C J, McCann, D J and Davies, R V (1986), 'The Margerison-McCann Team Management Resource', *International Journal of Manpower*, vol 7, no 2.

Margerison, C J and McCann, R (1990), *Team Management: Practical new approaches*, W H Allen.

Moxon, Peter (1993), *Building a Better Team*, Gower (includes 14 team-building activities).

Parker, Glenn M and Kropp, Richard P (1992), *Team Building: A sourcebook of activities for trainers*, Kogan Page (50 teambuilding activities).

Parker, Glenn M and Kropp, Richard P (1996), *50 Activities for Self-Directed Teams*, Gower.

Prior, John (ed) (1994), *Handbook of Training and Development*, Gower.

Stewart, Roger (ed) (forthcoming), *Handbook of Teams and Teamworking*, Gower.

Storey, Rod (1997), *The Team Working Activity Pack: 23 tried and tested activities to enhance team performance*, Fenman.

Woodcock, Mike (1989), *Team Development Manual*, Gower.

Woodcock, Mike and Francis, Dave (1997), *The Woodcock Francis Team Development Kit*, Gower.

Woodcock, Mike and Francis, Dave (1997), *25 Interventions for Improving Team Performance*, Gower.

Woodcock, Mike (1988), *50 Activities for Teambuilding*, Gower.

Transactional Analysis and NLP

Alder, Harry (1996), *NLP for Trainers: Communicating for excellence*, McGraw-Hill.

Bandler, Richard and Grinder, John (1979), *Frogs into Princes*, Real People Press (NLP).

Berne, Eric (1968), *Games People Play*, Penguin (TA).

Dimmick, Sally (1995), *Successful Communication through NLP*, Gower.

Garratt, Ted (1997), *The Effective Delivery of Training using NLP*, Kogan Page.

Harris, Thomas A (1973), *I'm OK, You're OK*, Pan (TA).

Hay, Julie (1992), *Transactional Analysis for Trainers*, McGraw-Hill.

Johnson, Roy (1996), *40 Activities for Training with NLP*, Gower.

Knight, Sue (1995), *NLP at Work*, Brealey.

Novey, Theodore B (1976), *TA for Management*, MCB.

Prior, John (ed) (1994), *Handbook of Training and Development*, Gower.

Seymour, J and O'Connor, J (1990), *Introducing NLP*, HarperCollins.

Seymour, J and O'Connor, J (1994), *Training with NLP*, HarperCollins.

Index